Errata

Errata
an examined life

George Steiner

Yale University Press   New Haven and London

First published in Great Britain in 1997 by
Weidenfeld & Nicholson. Published in the
United States in 1998 by Yale University
Press.

Set in Garamond type by
Keystone Typesetting, Inc.

Printed in the United States of America.
ISBN: 978-0-300-08095-7

Library of Congress Catalog Card Number:
97-80458

A catalogue record for this book is available
from the British Library.

The paper in this book meets the guidelines
for permanence and durability of the Com-
mittee on Production Guidelines for Book
Longevity of the Council on Library
Resources.

For Alexis and Monique Philonenko

1

Rain, particularly to a child, carries distinct smells and colors. Summer rains in the Tyrol are relentless. They have a morose, flogging insistence and come in deepening shades of dark green. At night, the drumming is one of mice on or just under the roof. Even daylight can be sodden. But it is the smell which, after sixty years, stays with me. Of drenched leather and hung game. Or, at moments, of tubers steaming under drowned mud. A world made boiled cabbage.

The summer was already ominous. A family holiday in the dark yet magical landscape of a country condemned. In those mid-1930s, Jew-hatred and a lust for reunification with Germany hung in the Austrian air. My father, who was convinced that catastrophe was imminent, and the gentile husband of my aunt still blandly optimistic, found conversation awkward. My mother and her fitfully hysterical sister sought to achieve an effect of normality. But the planned pastimes – swimming and boating on the lake, walks in the woods and hills – dissolved in the perpetual downpour. My impatience, my demands for entertainment in a cavernous chalet which was increasingly chill and, I imagine, mildewed, must have been pestilential. One morning, uncle Rudi drove into Salzburg. He brought back with him a small book in blue waxen covers.

It was a pictorial guide to coats of arms in the princely city and surrounding fiefs. Each blazon was reproduced in color, together with a brief historical notice as to the castle, family-domain, bishopric, or abbey which it identified. The little manual closed with a map marking the relevant sites, including ruins, and with a glossary of heraldic terms.

Even today, I can feel the pressure of wonder, the inward shock which this chance "pacifier" triggered. What is difficult to render in adult language is the combination, almost the fusion of delight and menace, of fascination and unease I experienced as I retreated to my room, the drains spitting under the rain-lashed eaves, and sat, hour after entranced hour, turning the pages, committing to memory the florid names of those towers, keeps, and high personages.

Though I could not, obviously, have defined or phrased it in any such way, that armorial primer overwhelmed me with a sense of the numberless specificity, of the minutiae, of the manifold singularity of the substance and forms of the world. Each coat of arms differed from every other. Each had its symbolic organization, motto, history, locale, and date wholly proper, wholly integral to itself. It "heralded" a unique, ultimately intractable fact of being. Within its quarterings, each graphic component, color, and pattern entailed its own prodigal signification. Heraldry often inserts coats of arms within coats of arms. The suggestive French designation of this device is a *mise en abyme*. My treasures included a magnifying glass. I pored over the details of geometric and "bestiary" shapes, the lozenges, diamonds, diagonal slashes of each emblem; over the helmeted crests and "supporters" crowning, flanking the diverse arms; over the precise number of tassels which graced a bishop's, an archbishop's, or a cardinal's armorials.

The notion which, in some visceral impact, tided over me and held me mesmerized was this: if there are in this obscure province of one small country (diminished Austria) so many coats of arms, each unique, how many must there be in Europe, across the globe? I do not recall what grasp I had, if any, of large numbers. But I do

remember that the word "millions" came to me and left me unnerved. How was any human being to see, to master this plurality?
Suddenly it came to me, in some sort of exultant but also appalled
revelation, that no inventory, no heraldic encyclopedia, no *summa*
of fabled beasts, inscriptions, chivalric hallmarks, however com-
pendious, could ever be *complete*. The opaque thrill and desolation
which came over me in that ill-lit and end-of-summer room on
the Wolfgangsee – was it, distantly, sexual? – has, in good part,
oriented my life.

I grew possessed by an intuition of the particular, of diversities
so numerous that no labor of classification and enumeration could
exhaust them. Each leaf differed from any other on each differing
tree (I rushed out in the deluge to assure myself of this elementary
and miraculous truth). Each blade of grass, each pebble on the
lake-shore was, eternally, "just so." No repetition of measurement,
however closely calibrated, in whatever controlled vacuum it was
carried out, could ever be perfectly the same. It would deviate by
some trillionth of an inch, by a nanosecond, by the breadth of a
hair – itself a teeming immensity – from any preceding measurement. I sat on my bed striving to hold my breath, knowing that
the next breath would signal a new beginning, that the past was already unrecapturable in its differential sequence. Did I guess that
there could be no perfect facsimile of anything, that the identical
word spoken twice, even in lightning-quick reiteration, was not
and could not be the same? (Much later, I was to learn that this un-
repeatability had preoccupied both Heraclitus and Kierkegaard.)

At that hour, in the days following, the totalities of personal
experience, of human contacts, of landscape around me became a
mosaic, each fragment at once luminous and resistant in its "quid-
dity" (the Scholastic term for integral presence revived by Gerard
Manley Hopkins). There could be, I knew, no finality to the

raindrops, to the number and variousness of the stars, to the books to be read, to the languages to be learned. The mosaic of the possible could, at any instant, be splintered and reassembled into new images and notions of meaning. The idiom of heraldry, those "gules" and "bars sinister," even if I could not yet make it out, must, I sensed, be only one among countless systems of discourse specifically tailored to the teeming diversity of human purposes, artifacts, representations, or concealment (I still recall the strange excitement I felt at the thought that a coat of arms could hide as well as reveal).

I set out, as many children do, to compile lists. Of monarchs and mythological heroes, of popes, of castles, of numinous dates, of operas – I had been taken to see *Figaro* at the neighboring Salzburg Festival. The wearied assurance of my parents that such lists already existed, that they could be looked up in any almanac or work of standard reference brought no solace. (My queries about anti-popes and how to include them visibly irritated my somewhat ceremonious and Catholic uncle.) The available indices of reality, be they a thousand pages thick, the atlases, the children's encyclope-dias, could never be exhaustively comprehensive. This or that item, perhaps the hidden key to the edifice, would be left out. There was simply too much to everything. Existence thronged and hummed with obstinate difference like the midges around the light-bulb. "Who can number the clouds in wisdom? Or who can stay the bottles of heaven?" (How did the writer of Job 38:37 already know about rains in the Salzkammergut?) I may not have cited the verse to myself in that drowned August, though the Old Testament was already a tutelary voice, but I did know of those bottles.

If the revelation of incommensurable "singleness" held me spellbound, it also generated fear. I would come back to the *mise en abyme* of one blazon within another, to that "setting in the abyss." I would consider a fathomless depth of differentiation, of non-identity, always incipient with the eventuality of chaos. How could the senses, how could the brain impose order and coherence on the kaleidoscope, on the *perpetuum mobile* of swarming existence? I harbored vague nightmares about the fact, revealed in the nature column of some newspaper, that a small corner of the Amazon forest was habitat to 30,000 rigorously distinct species of beetles. Gazing at, recopying with water-colors, the baronial or episcopal or civic arms, pondering the unlimited variations possible on formal and iconic motifs, I felt a peculiar dread. Detail could know no end.

A subtle queasiness emanates from such infinities. Greek classical sensibility flinched from irrational numbers and the incommensurable. My juvenile reflex was to attempt to devise a coat of arms, tabard, and heraldic pennants for one Sixtus von Falkenhorst, an imaginary prelate, bellicose and sensual, nesting in an almost inaccessible mountain eyrie, in whose central tower lodged the list of all lists, the *summa summarum* of all that is. This imbroglio of enchantment and terror proved consequential.

I have conducted my emotional, intellectual, and professional affairs in distrust of theory. So far as I am able, I can attach meaning to the concept of theory in the exact and, to some degree, applied sciences. These theoretical constructs demand crucial experiments for their verification or falsification. If refuted, they will be superseded. They can be mathematically or logically formalized. The invocation of "theory" in the humanities, in historical and social studies, in the evaluation of literature and the arts, seems to me mendacious. The humanities are susceptible neither to crucial experiments nor to verification (except on a material, documentary level). Our responses to them are narratives of intuition. In the unbounded dynamics of the semantic, in the flux of the meaningful, in the uncircumscribed interplay of interpretations, the only propositions are those of personal choice, of taste, of echoing affinity or deafness. There can be no refutations or disproofs in any theoretical sense. Coleridge does not refute Samuel Johnson; Picasso does not advance on Raphael. In humane letters, "theory" is nothing but intuition grown impatient.

My persuasion that the current triumph of the theoretical in literary, historical, sociological discourse is self-deception, that it enacts a failure of nerve in the face of the prestige of the sciences, goes back to those irreducibly individual coats of arms which leapt to unsettling life for me in that summer of 1936. Later, I was to learn that formal rules and exact conventions do underlie the code, the quarterings of heraldry, that there are systematic figurations and allegories. If one so wishes, a "theoretical" reading of armorial meanings is possible. To me, however, this abstract program cannot alter or communicate the life-force of individuation. It cannot substantiate the existential circumstance – temporal, familial, psychological – of the *dramatis persona* who bore that shield. No two lions rampant roar the same saga. Possessed by Blake's "holiness of the minute particular," by the dizzying knowledge that there are in chess, after the initial five moves, more possibilities than atoms in the universe, I have found myself isolated from the now-dominant turn to theory. The games played in deconstruction, in post-modernism, in the imposition on the study of history and society of metamathematical models (the mathematics being, often, pretentiously naïve) largely condition the climate of academic-critical pursuits. The theoreticians in power consider my own work, if they consider it at all, as archaic impressionism. As heraldry.

But art and poetry will always give to universals "a local habitation and a name." They have made the particular, even the minute, inviolable. Nowhere more so than in Canto IV of Pope's *The Rape of the Lock:*

A constant Vapour o'er the palace flies;
Strange phantoms rising as the mists arise;
Dreadful, as hermit's dreams in haunted shades,
Or bright, as visions of expiring maids.
Now glaring fiends, and snakes on rolling spires,
Pale spectres, gaping tombs, and purple fires:
Now lakes of liquid gold, Elysian scenes,
And crystal domes, and Angels in machines.

Unnumber'd throngs on ev'ry side are seen,
Of bodies chang'd to various forms of Spleen.
Here living Tea-pots stand, one arm held out,
One bent; the handle this, and that the spout:
A Pipkin there, like Homer's Tripod walks;
Here sighs a Jar, and there a Goose-pye talks;
Men prove with child, as pow'rful fancy works,
And maids turn'd bottles, call aloud for corks.

That last couplet cries out, doubtless, for reduction to the psycho-analytic. Yet how little of its surrealistic magic such reduction can theorize. Pope's ironic self-subversions can, indeed, be grist for a deconstructive mill. Ground to theoretical dust, what have they yielded of their nightmare-charm? The most penetrating gloss on this passage is Beardsley's illustration in which, if not God, the devil lies in the detail. Ask any child whether that "living Tea-pot" can suffer deconstruction, whether theory can arrest that walking pipkin.

2

How can a human voice cast a huge, sickening shadow? On short waves, the wireless chirped and often dissolved in bursts of static. But Hitler's speeches, when broadcast, punctuated my childhood (whence, so many years later, *The Portage to San Cristobal of A.H.*). My father would bend close to the wireless, straining to hear. We were in Paris, where I was born in 1929. One of the doctors assisting at my awkward birth then returned to Louisiana to assassinate Huey Long. History was always in attendance.

My parents had left Vienna in 1924. From meager circumstances, from a Czech-Austrian milieu still in reach of the ghetto, my father had risen to meteoric eminence. Anti-semitic Vienna, the cradle of Nazism, was, in certain respects, a liberal meritocracy. He had secured a senior legal position in the Austrian Central Bank, with *fiacre* (a use of a carriage and horses). A brilliant career lay before the youthful *Herr Doktor*. With grim clairvoyance, my father perceived the nearing disaster. A systematic, doctrinal Jew-hatred seethed and stank below the glittering liberalities of Viennese culture. The world of Freud, of Mahler, of Wittgenstein was also that of Mayor Lueger, Hitler's exemplar. At their lunatic source, Nazism and the "final solution" are Austrian rather than German reflexes. Like his friend out of Galicia, one Lewis Namier, my father dreamt of England. For the eastern and central European Jewish intelligentsia, the career of Disraeli had assumed a mythical, talismanic aura. But he suffered from rheumatic fevers, and the medical sagacity of the day held France to be the milder climate. So Paris it was, and a new start under strained circumstances (my mother, Viennese to her fingertips, lamented this seemingly irrational move). And to the end of his days, my father never felt at home among what he judged to be the arrogant chauvinism, the frivolities, the myopia of French politics, finance, and society. He would mutter under his breath (unjustly) that all nationalities would sell you their mothers, but the French delivered.

Of fragile physique, my father was compounded of formidable will and intellect. He found a surprisingly large portion of mankind unacceptable. Sloppiness, lies (even "white" ones), and evasions of reality infuriated him. He lacked the arts of forgiveness. His contributions to the skills of international investment banking, to the techniques of corporate finance in the period between the wars are on record. His Zionism had the ardor of one who knew, even at the outset, that he would not emigrate to Palestine. His bookplate shows a bark, a seven-branched candelabrum at its bow, approaching Jerusalem. But the holy city remains on the far horizon. Papa embodied, as did every corner of our Paris home, the tenor, the prodigality and glow of Jewish-European and Central European emancipation. The horrors which reduced this liberal humaneness and vision to ashes have distorted remembrance. Evocations of the Shoah have, tragically, privileged the remembrance of prior suffering, particularly throughout eastern Europe. The proud Judaism of my father was, like that of an Einstein or a Freud, one of messianic agnosticism. It breathed rationality, the promise of the Enlightenment and tolerance. It owed as much to Voltaire as it did to Spinoza. High holidays, notably the Day of Atonement, were observed not for prescriptive or theological motives, but as a yearly summons to identity, to a homeland in millennial time.

By virtue of what was to become an unbearable paradox, this Judaism of secular hope looked to German philosophy, literature, scholarship, and music for its talismanic guarantees. German metaphysics and cultural criticism, from Kant to Schopenhauer and Nietzsche, the classics of German-language poetry and drama, the master-historians such as Ranke, Mommsen, and Gregorovius crowded the shelves of my father's library. As did first editions of Heine, in whose mordant wit, in whose torn and ambiguous destiny, in whose unhoused virtuosity in both German and French, my father saw the prophetic mirror of modern European Judaism. Like so many German, Austrian, and Central European Jews, my father was immersed in Wagner. During his very brief spell under arms in Vienna in 1914, he had ridden a horse named Lohengrin; he had then married a woman called Elsa. It was, however, the whole legacy of German-Austrian music, it was Mozart, Beethoven, Schubert, Hugo Wolf, and Mahler who filled the house. As a very young child, at the edge of bedtime and through a crack in the living-room door, I was sometimes allowed to hear chamber-music, a *Lieder*-recital, being performed by musicians invited into our home. They were, increasingly, refugees in desolate plight. Yet even in the thickening political twilight, a Schubert song, a Schumann study could light up my father's haunted mien. When concessions had to be made to encroaching reality, my father gave them an ironic touch: recordings of Wagner were now played in French.

Only in the posthumously published letters of Gershom Scholem have I come across the same note of helpless clear-sightedness and warning. Over and over, even prior to 1933, my father labored to warn, to alert, to awaken to refuge not only those whom he and my mother had left behind in Prague or in Vienna, but the French political-military establishment with which his international dealings had brought him into contact. His "pessimism," his "alarmist prognostications" elicited only officious dismissal or hostility. Family and friends refused to move. One could come to reasonable terms with Herr Hitler. The unpleasantness would soon pass. The age of pogroms was over. In diplomatic and ministerial circles, my father was regarded as a tedious Cassandra, prone to well-known traits of Jewish hysteria. Papa lived those rancid 1930s like a man trapped in cobwebs, lashing out and sick at heart. There was also, however, a more private and constant regret.

His own studies in law and economic theory had been of exceptional strength. He had published monographs on the utopian economics of Saint-Simon and on the Austrian banking crises of the later nineteenth century. The absolute need to support various less-qualified members of his family, the collapse of the dual monarchy, and the aftermath of the First World War had thrust him into finance. He respected the importance and the technical ingenuities of his craft, but cultivated scant regard for most of those who practiced it. (One of the few contemporaries he acknowledged as preeminent, also in integrity, and whom he came, in certain outward gestures and in tone to resemble, was Siegmund Warburg.) My father's innermost passions lay elsewhere. His uncertain health had barred him from medical studies. He turned to intellectual history, to the history and philosophic aspects of biology. His learning was extensive and exact. His appetite for languages remained unquenched to the very end (he was systematically acquiring Russian at the time of his death). Investment banking occupied most of his outward existence. At the core, it left him almost indifferent. From this tension came his uncompromising resolve that his son should know next to nothing of his father's profession. This partition could reach absurd lengths: "I would rather that you did not know the difference between a bond and a share." I was to be a teacher and a thorough scholar. On this last point, I have failed him.

Why this elevation of the teacher-scholar rather than, say, the artist, the writer, or the performer in a sensibility so responsive to music, literature, and the arts? There was scarcely a museum in Paris and, later, in New York, to which he did not take me on a Saturday. It is in this instinctive preference for teaching and learning, for the discovery and transmission of the truth that my father, in his aching stoicism, was most profoundly Jewish. Like Islam, Judaism is iconoclastic. It fears the image, it distrusts the metaphor. Emancipated Judaism delights in the performing artist, especially the musician. It has produced masters of stage and film. Yet even to this day, when it informs so much of American literature, when it can look to a Kafka, a Proust, a Mandelstam, or a Paul Celan, Judaism is not altogether at ease with the poetics of invention (*fabulation*), with the mustard-seed of "falsehood" or fiction, with the rivalry to God the creator inherent in the arts. Given the limitless wonders of the created universe, when there is such wealth of actual being to be recorded and grasped by reason, when there is history to be untangled, law to be clarified, science to be furthered, is the devising of fictions, of mimesis a truly responsible, a genuinely adult pursuit? Freud, for one, did not think so. Fictions were to be outgrown as man ripened into the "reality principle." Somewhere in my father's restless spirit a comparable doubt may have nagged. Even the most Voltairean, perhaps atheistic – I do not know – of Jews knows that the word *rabbi* simply means "teacher."

Only later did I come to realize the investment of hope against hope, of watchful inventiveness, which my father made in educating me. This, during years of private and public torment, when the bitter need to find some future for us as Nazism drew near, left him emotionally and physically worn out. I marvel still at the loving astuteness of his devices. No new book was allowed me till I had written down for his inspection a précis of the one I had just read. If I had not understood this or that passage – my father's choices and suggestions were aimed carefully above my head – I was to read it to him out loud. Often the voice clears up a text. If misunderstanding persisted, I was to copy the relevant bit in my own writing. At which move, it would usually surrender its lode.

Though I was hardly aware of the design, my reading was held in balance between French, English, and German. My upbringing was totally trilingual, and the background always polyglot. My radiant Mama would habitually begin a sentence in one tongue and end it in another. Once a week, a diminutive Scottish lady appeared to read Shakespeare to and with me. I entered that world, I am not certain why, via *Richard II*. Adroitly, the first speech I was made to learn by heart was not that of Gaunt, but Mowbray's farewell, with its mordant music of exile. A refugee scholar coached me in Greek and Latin. He exhaled an odor of reduced soap and sorrow.

I could not yet conceive of, let alone articulate, the creed at work in my father's purpose. I accepted, with unquestioning zest, the idea that study and a hunger for understanding were the most natural, the determinant ideals. Consciously or not, the skeptical ironist had set out for his son a secular Talmud. I was to learn how to read, how to internalize word and commentary in the hope, however chancy, that I might one day add to that commentary, to the survival of the text, a further hint of light. My childhood was made a demanding festival.

The confirmation occurred one late winter evening, not long

before my sixth birthday. My father had, in broad strokes, told me the story of the *Iliad.* He had kept the book itself out of my impatient reach. Now he opened it before us in the translation by Johann-Heinrich Voss of 1793. Papa turned to Book XXI. Crazed by the death of his beloved Patroclus, Achilles is butchering the fleeing Trojans. Nothing can impede his homicidal fury. One of Priam's sons crosses his path. The wretched Lycaon has just returned from Lemnos to help defend his father's imperiled city. Earlier, Achilles had captured him and sold him into slavery at Lemnos, thus ironically consigning him to safety. But Lycaon is back. Now the appalled youth recognizes the blind horror storming at him. I cite Robert Fagles's version (1990):

> . . . He ducked, ran under the hurl
> And seized Achilles' knees as the spear shot past his back
> and stuck in the earth, still starved for human flesh.
> And begging now, one hand clutching Achilles' knees,
> the other gripping the spear, holding for dear life,
> Lycaon burst out with a winging prayer: "Achilles!
> I grasp your knees – respect me, show me mercy!
> I am your suppliant, Prince, you must respect me!"

Lycaon's abject terror mounts:

> "And it's just twelve days that I've been home in Troy –
> all I've suffered! But now, again, some murderous fate
> has placed me in your hands, your prisoner twice over –
> Father Zeus must hate me, giving me back to you!
> Ah, to a short life you bore me, mother – mother . . ."

One final, pathetic sophistry:

"Listen, this too, take it to heart, I beg you —
don't kill me! I'm not from the same womb as Hector,
Hector who killed your friend, your strong, *gentle* friend!"

At which line, my father stopped with an air of considered help-
lessness. What, in God's name, happens next? I must have been
shaking with excited frustration, shaking. Ah, said Papa, there was
a gap in Voss's translation, indeed in all available translations. To
be sure, there *was* the original, Homer's Greek, which lay open on
the table, together with a lexicon and introductory grammar.
Should we try and decipher the burning passage for ourselves? It
was not, my father added, difficult Greek. Perhaps we could manage Achilles' reply. And he took my finger, placing it on the appropriate Greek words:

. . . "Fool,
don't talk to me of ransom. No more speeches.
Before Patroclus met his day of destiny, true,
it warmed my heart a bit to spare some Trojans:
droves I took alive and auctioned off as slaves.
But now not a single Trojan flees his death,
not one the gods hand over to me before your gates,
none of all the Trojans, sons of Priam least of all!
Come, friend, you too must die. Why moan about it so?
Even Patroclus died, a far, far better man than you.
And look, you see how handsome and powerful I am?
The son of a great man, the mother who gave me life
a deathless goddess. But even for me, I tell you,
death and the strong force of fate are waiting.
There will come a dawn or sunset or high noon
when a man will take my life in battle too —

flinging a spear perhaps
or whipping a deadly arrow off his bow."

Whereupon, Achilles slaughters the kneeling Lycaon.

My father read the Greek several times over. He made me mouth the syllables after him. Dictionary and grammar flew open. Like the lineaments of a brightly colored mosaic lying under sand, when you pour water on it, the words, the formulaic phrases, took on form and meaning for me. Word by sung word, verse by verse. I recall graphically the rush of wonder, of a child's consciousness troubled and uncertainly ripened, by that single word "friend" in the midst of the death-sentence: "Come, *friend,* you too must die." And by the enormity, so far as I could gauge it, of the question: "Why moan about it so?" Very slowly, allowing me his treasured Waterman pen, my father let me trace some of the Greek letters and accents.

Tapping my excitement (it would be some time before I discovered that translations of Homer did *not* omit the most thrilling bits), Papa made a further proposal, as in passing: "Shall we learn some lines from this episode by heart?" So that the serene inhumanity of Achilles' message, its soft terror, would never leave us. Who could tell, moreover, what I might find on my night-table when going back to my room? I raced. And found my first Homer. Perhaps the rest has been a foot-note to that hour.

The *Iliad* and the *Odyssey* have been lifelong companions. I have tried to honor a debt of love by studying and writing about Homer. My daughter, Deborah, is an exact and illuminating philologist, but my amateur (*amatore,* "the lover") intuition tells me that the editor who compiled the oral fragments of the Troy-saga into a unified text, into our *Iliad,* was, late in his life, the author of the *Odyssey.* The genius of the two works differs as does a novel from a supreme ballad. We hear in the *Odyssey* a skepticism, sometimes playful, sometimes tragic (notably during the dialogue with Achilles in Hades), as to the unexamined exaltation of murderous heroism in the *Iliad*. A searching, in some sense domestic, sensibility looks back on the earlier epic.

I have collected English-language translations of the Homeric epics and hymns. These run into the hundreds. Of all my work, *Homer in English,* a selection from this trove published in 1996, has brought me the most immediate pleasure. It tells of peregrine years among book-barns, auctions, Charing Cross Road stalls, and dusty boxes. It recalls sudden finds – a first edition of Hobbes's "Homer" after a quarter century in pursuit; the purchase, much beyond reasonable means, of the rare first issue of Lamb's tales from the *Odyssey,* and of the original publication of Pound's first *Canto,* the Circe-*canto* in mint condition, from under a grotty pile of film-weeklies. There is in this anthology a history of the language from Caxton to Walcott, from Chaucer to Tom Gunn; a chronicle of Anglo-American consciousness and self-consciousness as the radioactive tracer of the Homeric lights its fabric from generation to generation. And there is, for me, in every page a spoor of my father's voice.

Lycaon's fatal exchange with Achilles concentrates much of what perception is granted us as to the limits of human speech in the face of death. To carry this narrative with one (to learn it by heart) is to possess a turning-fork against illusion. Together with Tolstoy's "Ivan Ilitch" (Tolstoy is one of our pre-eminent readers of the *Iliad*), Achilles' fatalism – its momentary tenderness, blank as the eyes of archaic Greek figures – instructs us of our triviality. Achilles is the lucid instrument of that extinction which inhabits life. Tougher than Falstaff's jaunty edict that we all owe God a life, is Achilles' reminder that we all owe death a life. A terrible clarity is

born. Christopher Logue hears the light from Achilles' helmet
"screaming across three thousand years." Because he expressly includes his own imminent death in that of the hysterical boy, Achilles conveys an enigmatic forgiveness: where he concurs with otherwise unendurable reality, man forgives life, forgives the human
condition, for being the indifferent, end-stopped thing it is.

There are numerous such "summations" in the two sagas. An
attempt at understanding, as best we can, the nature of representa-
tion and remembrance, of fact and fiction, will take its source at
the court of the Phaeacians, in Book VIII of the *Odyssey*. Demodocus the blind minstrel (sight has become insight) sings to the
assembled lords and their unknown guest. He sings of the battles
before Troy and of Odysseus. Hearing himself sung, the voyager
succumbs to tears. Not only, I believe, because of the manifest
pathos of recollection, not only because the somber destinies of his
erstwhile companions-at-arms are brought home to him. But,
more devastatingly, because the minstrel's recital compels Odysseus to confront the "unmaking," the dissemination of his own
living self. He has passed already into the insubstantial everlasting-
ness of fiction. He has been emptied into legend. No poetics after
Homer, no philosophic inquiry into the status of the imaginary
with reference to the empirical, cuts deeper. There are, in literature and the arts, other privileged acts of mirroring inward, such as
the snatches from *Figaro* played by the house-band at Don Gio-
vanni's last supper, or such as the narrator's return to Venice in
Proust. None is richer or more complex than Odysseus' audition
of Demodocus.

Or consider the night-meeting of Priam and Achilles in Book
XXIV of the *Iliad*. The father is begging the body of his son Hector
from his killer. He places his lips on "those man-murdering hands."
Every line is – I can put it no other way – measureless to our

response. Once more, the center is one of implacable truth to life (to death). Both men have wept piteously. Achilles knows that his triumph over Hector entails his own doom as well as that of Priam's many-towered city. He will know no home-coming to his own aged sire. But now, in that tent of death, it is time to eat. No grief, however monumental, altogether abolishes hunger. Achilles reminds Priam that after the slaying of all her children, Niobe "fell to meat" (as a Jacobean translator puts it). Would Shakespeare have ventured this touch? Tolstoy understood it perfectly.

The dimensions implicit here are those of the "classic." What is a "classic"? What is the agency of its persistence across time, languages, and altering societies? What authorizes the tap, tap of sightless Homer's white cane in Joyce's Dublin?

I define a "classic," in literature, in music, in the arts, in philosophic argument, as a signifying form which "reads" us. It reads us more than we read (listen to, perceive) it. There is nothing paradoxical, let alone mystical, in this definition. Each time we engage with it, the classic will question us. It will challenge our resources of consciousness and intellect, of mind and body (so much of primary aesthetic and even intellectual response is bodily). The classic will ask of us: "have you understood?"; "have you re-imagined responsibly?"; "are you prepared to act upon the questions, upon the potentialities of transformed, enriched being which I have posed?"

Let us take these queries in turn.

The arts of understanding (hermeneutics) are as manifold as their objects. Signs are unbounded; both in combinatorial modes and in potentialities of significance. There is nothing more unnerving in the human condition than the fact that we can mean and/or say *anything*. This semantic unboundedness comports an uncircumscribed variousness of approaches to interpretation. In the case of language, of any form of discourse or text, of any speech-act, words seek out words. There is no *a priori* limit to the ways in which this search, this quest for meaning, can be conducted. The words which we use to elucidate or paraphrase or interpret ("translate") those of the message, of the text before us, share with that message or text a radical undecidability. They are, as linguistics after Saussure has taught us, arbitrary, conventional markers. A "horse" is no more like a horse than is a *cheval.* A formal freedom attaches to the sign.

On the other hand, the sign is encrusted, beyond lexical-grammatical definition, with phonetic, historical, social, idiomatic overtones and undertones. It carries with it connotations, associations, previous usages, tonal, and even graphic, pictorial values and suggestions (the look, the "shape" of words). Except in mathematical and logically formal notations, the semantic unit is never totally neutral or totally "in play" (Wittgenstein's "language-games"). Nevertheless, text and interpretation or decipherment are reciprocally incommensurable. They act on each other via processes which also act on themselves. Every explanation, every critical-interpretative proposition, is another text.

This is why Western literacy, in its Hebraic-Hellenic matrix, has, until very recently, been one of commentary, of commentary on commentary almost *ad infinitum.* (Of the "making of books" and of books on books there is, as Ecclesiastes observes, no end.) To listen to words, to read them, is, consciously or not, to reach out for context, for placement in a meaningful whole. Here again, in any strict sense (and just what is "a strict sense"?) the unlimited prevails. The informing context of any single sentence in, say, Flaubert's *Madame Bovary,* is that of the immediate paragraph, of the surrounding chapter, of the entire novel. It is also that of the state of the French language at Flaubert's time and place, of the history of French society, and of the ideologies, politics, colloquial associations, and terrain of implicit and explicit reference, which press on, which perhaps subvert or ironize, the words, the turns of phrase in that particular sentence. The stone strikes the water and concentric circles ripple outward to open-ended horizons. Context, without which there can be neither meaning nor understanding, is the world.

Hence, in my opinion, the falsehood of post-structuralist and deconstructionist claims that "there is nothing outside the text," that discourse is an autonomous game continually effacing and emptying of referential validation its own possible intent and significance. Meaning is as close-knit to circumstance, to perceived realities (however conjectural and transient these are), as is our body. Attempts at understanding, at "reading well," at responsive reception are, at all times, historical, social, and ideological. We cannot "hear" Homer as did his first audience. It may even be, as Borges asserts, that in the late twentieth century, the *Odyssey* ought to be dated after Joyce's *Ulysses*. But it is just these vital determinants of context which render absurd the postulate of meaning without external and often non-linguistic reference.

It is the cumulative, argumentative, self-correcting enterprise of vision and revision which makes every proposal of understanding, every "decoding" and interpretation (these two being strictly inseparable) tentative. It is precisely the identifying attribute of trivia, of ephemeral work, be it in music, literature, or the arts, that it can be classed and understood once and for all. In a perfectly rational and pragmatic sense, a serious act of signification – verbal, imaged, tonal – is inexhaustible to interpretative summation. It cannot be anatomized or held in fixed place. Each and every reading, in the larger sense of the term, each and every hermeneutic-critical mapping, remains provisional, incomplete and possibly erroneous.

With regard to language, no dictionary is final. Words alter their definitions and range – their *Sprachfeld,* as German puts it vividly – throughout the history of the language, across regions, age-groups, and levels of society. Grammar, which is the nerve of thought, has its rich history, its dialectical tensions between correctness (a highly political, empowered notion) and subversion, between inheritance and innovation. Any motion of meaning in human utterance or expression will occur, will "come to pass" in the full temporal connotations of this biblical phrase, between convention and anarchy, between cliché and creation. The possibilities of variation, of mutation are formally endless. As are those of explicative reception and response. The instruments range from archaeology and the epigraphic restoration of mutilated texts all the way to the psychoanalytic, from scriptural exegesis and the interlinear gloss to the fantastications of deconstruction, from analyses of a syntaxic-logical order to the socio-historical interpretations and critiques offered by Thomism or by Marxism. The carnival of understanding and judgment is open to all. But even the most manifold, the most rigorously systematic "setting out" of a text, of the meanings of its meaning, will never finalize its object. The classic eludes any final decidability.

This is the crux. A master-reader (or viewer or listener) equipped, in the case of literature, with linguist-historical knowledge, ideally sensitive to the polysemic, metamorphic lives of language, inspiredly intuitive in his or her empathy – a Coleridge reading Wordsworth, a Karl Barth glossing Romans, a Mandelstam responding to Dante – will come only "so near." The ultimate life-force of the poem or prose being elucidated, its power against time, will remain integral. No hermeneutic is equivalent to its object. No restatement, via analytic "dissection," paraphrase, or emotive description, can replace the original (in the ephemeral, in the functional, such substitution lies to hand).

The proof is with music. The sum of understanding resides in further performance. Thus interpretation and criticism are, at their most honest, more or less suggestive, enriching narrations of personal, always provisional encounters. It is this provisional subjectivity, this persistent need for reconsideration and amendment, which does give a certain legitimacy to the deconstructionalist project. No external ruling, be it the trope of divine revelation, be it the author's express dictum, can guarantee interpretation. Nor can consensus, itself always partial or temporary, across "canonic" and general literacy. It is empirically possible that we are getting it wrong, whatever our labors and unanimities. It is logically conceivable that the text before us signifies *nothing,* that it purposes or enacts non-sense. It is just possible that the author seeks to ironize his work into playful ghostliness. But the assumptions underlying this non-reading, this dissemination into the void, are themselves arbitrary and rooted substantively in the language in which they are expressed (deconstructionists and post-modernists pour out prolix treatises). I have, throughout my work, most explicitly in *Real Presences* (1989), proposed the contrary wager: on the relations, however opaque, of word to world, on intentionalities, however difficult to unravel, in texts, in works of art, soliciting recognition. Here, as so often in our muddled being, the vital grain, the life-pattern is that of common sense.

But I repeat: all understanding falls short. It is as if the poem, the painting, the sonata drew around itself a last circle, a space for inviolate autonomy. I define the classic as that around which this space is perennially fruitful. It questions us. It demands that we try again. It makes of our misprisions, of our partialities and disagreements not a relativistic chaos, an "anything goes," but a deepening. Worthwhile interpretations, criticism to be taken seriously, are those which make their limitations, their defeats visible. In turn, this visibility helps make manifest the inexhaustibility of the object. The Bush burned brighter because its interpreter was not allowed too near.

When we endeavor to answer to a classic with whatever skills, scruples, and ordered feelings we have at our disposal, when we strive to make even our errors in some manner insightful, we practice what I call *philology*. The roots of words go to the heart of things: "philology" contains both "love" and the *logos*. It tells of the dialogue initiated not so much by ourselves as by the poem, the sculpture, the fugue, or the philosophic text confronting us.

After partial understanding, after philology but inseparable from it, comes answerability. Modes of response are as various as those of interpretation. At the privileged edge of immediacy, interpretation takes on a twofold meaning. The executant interprets a musical score when and as he performs it. The producer and actors interpret *Hamlet* as they stage it. Every musical performance, every staging of a play, is an act of pure hermeneutics, an explicative figuration of meanings. Conductors, directors in the theater, communicative readers of poetry, are our first-line respondents and interpreters. So is the translator. However pedestrian or exalted, however routine or re-creative, a translation is always a primary thrust of understanding. The translator is also called "the interpreter." He strives to transmit the sense of the source. A mirror looks into a mirror, exchanging what it can of light. Translation can modulate into a wealth of responsive genres, of "answerings." These include parody, thematic variations, travesty, pastiche, and innumerable modes of adaptation (*Hamlet* in modern dress, in ballet, in opera, in tone-poems, in paintings, on ice). Indeed, the

structure of theme and variation appears to be seminal in our
Western intellectual and aesthetic practice. "Odysseys" are legion
from Homer to Joyce and Derek Walcott. There have been a
dozen "Antigones" this century. Oedipus cast his ever-renewed
(reinterpreted) shadow from Sophocles to Freud. In its mimetic,
decomposing, satiric, or pathetic reprises, the art of Picasso is an
index to that of the past. We have no subtler a reader of Velasquez
or of Ingres than Picasso; no more enlightening respondent to
Goya than Manet; no truer criticism of *Madame Bovary* than
Anna Karenina. It is the imperious license of the classic to demand,
to generate active reply ("replay"), even where that activity is, as
my father taught me, only that of learning by heart. In respect of
literature or music, to memorize is to give a first answer. It is to
begin to apprehend what the ancient thinkers and poets meant
when they proclaimed Memory to be the mother of the Muses.
Learning by heart is philology in action. Or to put it another way,
one reads a classic with a pencil in hand.

The third demand made of us by serious art, music, literature,
or philosophy is the most difficult to formulate, let alone satisfy.
Any experience modifies consciousness. Be it subliminal or trau-
matic, there is no psychic or physical-material happening which
does not alter the complex of our identity. In the flux of the instan-
taneous, the impact, like that of the charged particles streaming
through our planet, is infinitesimal and unperceived. But personal
being is process; it is in perpetual change. Being disinterested and
so often entirely unexpected – the painting seen suddenly on a
wall or in a gallery, the melody which possesses our bodily motion
and memory unbidden, the poem or novel or play which, as it
were, lay in ambush – the meeting, the collision between awareness and signifying form, between perception and the aesthetic, is
among the most powerful. It can transmute us. This is overwhelm-

ingly true of music, though the nature and *modus operandi* of seizure by music is little understood. The German word *Stimmung*, meaning "mood" and "state of being," also encapsulates "voice" and "tuning." We are "tuned" by the music that possesses us. But analogous dynamics are at work in our spontaneous passions (schoolchildren speak, tellingly, of "a craze") or distaste for this or that work of literature or the arts. Indifference is an enigmatic gray zone. The concatenations of strictly private-personal antennae, past experience or training, more or less avowed expectations, social-cultural conventions with some momentary inclination (*Stimmung*) or accidental circumstance, elude us. But the "experience-act" and its effects on us are unmistakable.

Pace Keats, all messages, all shapings of significance, verbal, representational, in the widest sense, musical, do have "a palpable design upon us." They ask to be heard, they demand understanding, where neither reception nor interpretation can ever be neutral. The "design upon us" can be trivial and meretricious as it is in, say, advertisement, pulp fiction, pornography, or tea-dance airs. It can be pedagogic, a nearly limitless range which extends from the humblest of manuals and primers to Socrates' apologia or the Sermon on the Mount. The message can be that of intended persuasion (rhetoric), of ethical, political, ideological propaganda and conversion. The "palpable design" of philosophy is clarification, a systematic house-cleaning in the lumber-room of the mind. Instruction, affliction, consolation, as these spring from literature and the arts, are designs, perhaps secondary, but no less purposed than are those of the logician, advocate, or preacher. The hold on us of the classic, the demands and questions it puts to us, are at once the subtlest and most urgent.

Kafka proclaimed, with characteristic extremity, that we need not waste our time on books which do not come on us like an ice-axe, shattering what is frozen inside our skulls and spirit. His own writings justify this absolutism. To phrase it more calmly: the major text, work of art, musical composition, the "news that stays new" (Ezra Pound), asks not only for understanding reception. It demands *reaction*. We are meant to act "anew," to translate echoing response and interpretation into conduct. Hermeneutics share a common border with ethics. To read Plato or Pascal or Tolstoy "classically" is to attempt a new and different life. It is, as Dante postulates explicitly, to enter on a *vita nuova*. In most art and literature, this summons is non-systematic. It remains implicit or enacted within the form. The play, the fiction, the Cézanne still-life so complicates, so dislocates from banality, so quickens our movements inward (Dante's *moto spirituale*) and our turn to the world, that we differ from before. The strata, the landscape of our perceptions have been, minutely or as by an earthquake, realigned.

Such dislocation can be unsettling, even painful. Hence the exasperated resistance to much of modern art, music, poetry; to the atonal and the non-representational. Or it can prove exultant, like the cool of a storm after stillness. Normally, the process of change is gradual. Imperceptibly, as it were, we come to notice that the meeting with the text has modified our experience of previous texts; that we no longer observe familiar objects or paintings as we did before; that music sounds otherwise. Proust is the unsurpassed witness to these inward earth-tremors. If there is in ourselves sufficient room for ripening, sufficient openness to eventuality, these mutations of audition, of vision, of cognition, these new imports into remembrance and aspiration, will translate into action. It is the central attribute and paradox of the classic that its commandments are liberating. The core of response, of reaction is one of compelled freedom.

Exposure, from early childhood, to these ordinances of excel-

lence, the desire to share with others the answerability and transmission in time without which the classic falls silent, made of me
exactly what my father intended: a teacher. The bidding of the
archaic torso of Apollo in Rilke's famous poem, "Change your
life," has been for me at the heart of meaning. I have been closest
to it when I have failed (this is, I know, the theological dilemma
par excellence).

The cost (I will come back to it) of this early incision of the
classical into my existence has been considerable. In music, my
joys do include the very modern, the sharply contemporary. By the
most *avant-garde* and experimental arts – the cloven calves, the
bricks on the museum floor – I have been numbed. The cardinal
role of the ephemeral, of the populist, of such media as photogra-
phy in our culture has, too often, passed me by. I delight in, but
have not internalized adequately, the authority of the cinema –
probably the major form in the twentieth century. These myopias,
moreover, are grounded in a larger *malaise*. Having been schooled
so young and insistently in the worship (the word is hardly exag-
gerated) of the classic, I came to ask myself whether our current
cultural, intellectual situation is not that of an afterword, of a
more or less confused epilogue. Will there come again a Plato or
a Mozart, a Shakespeare or a Rembrandt, a *Divine Comedy* or a
Critique of Pure Judgement? Logically, this is a silly question. The
next Michelangelo can be born tomorrow; or may be at his labors
today, in the next street. Why should there not be a Caribbean
Proust, a Beethoven out of Africa? But do we honestly believe in
this advent? Or is there substance to a sense of twilight? I want to
return to this difficult problem.

One point is clear. When he construed for me, when he made
me parse and commit to memory Achilles' statement that men

(and women) exceedingly more gifted, more necessary than we are must die (often very young and in utter waste or injustice); when he made me attend closely to Achilles' axiom that our own death has its prescribed morning, noon, or nightfall, my father sought to spare me certain stupidities.

3

During the war years, the French *Lycée* in Manhattan was a cauldron. It miniaturized all too faithfully the confused hatreds and divisions of the home country. The sons and daughters of diplomats, colonial servants, and military personnel loyal to the Vichy regime mingled with the children of exiles, of Jewish refugees, and of European families variously stranded in the New World. Some of the teachers were highly qualified, even eminent scholars who had been at universities but were now dependent on whatever employment they could find. Others were indifferent remnants exhibiting a mien of private or professional decrepitude. The head was a vaguely elegant, spectral personage, fascinated by minor literary classics (such as the works of Pierre Loti) and unconvinced as to the innocence of Captain Dreyfus. News of German triumphs and Vichy acquiescence, of resistance and early Gaullist stirrings, seeped through the class-rooms and corridors, like draughts, fetid or fresh, under a door. Till mid-1944, the official line was collaborationist. Pro-Pétain instructors and pupils had frequent occasions for more or less muted rejoicing (America was, after all, at war around them). After that, the winds veered with cynical abruptness. I recall the morning on which a Cross of Lorraine, strictly banned hitherto, made its opportune appearance on the assembly-room wall. The "Marseillaise" was intoned at full throat.

The realities of occupation and resistance had reached into our doll-house lives. Lying about their age, two students in the class above mine managed to get back to France via Mexico. They perished in the sadistic Waffen-SS massacres which followed on the premature uprising in the Vercors. *Monsieur le directeur* assumed an even ghostlier air than usual when he read out their names to us in censorious sorrow. Yet embroiled and cynical as the atmosphere and rhetoric were, the *Lycée* was, perhaps for that very reason, often electrifying. An unforgiving adulthood, an enormity of history, pressed on us. Particularly on the Jewish children, some of whom had left their families behind. It must have been in late 1944 or early 1945 when, in a moment of conspiratorial imbecility, I whispered to a class-mate what my father had begun to infer as to the "final solution." I shall never forget her outcry and the way she sought to scratch my face. That afternoon, after classes, we sat in mutual loathing and fear copying lines. Out of Virgil.

This was the point. French secondary schooling, assuredly at that date, turned on high literacy. It pivoted on the reading, *explication de texte,* and recitation, partly by heart, of the ancient classics and of French epic, poetry, and drama. The sovereignty of language, of poetic and oratorical style, was drummed from an early age into one's more or less receptive skull. French is, even in its lyricism, a public medium (the language has no exact term for "privacy"). It prizes eloquence to excess. Even in the erotic, the innervation by formal rhetoric, by conventions of verbal splendor, is pervasive. French deaths can be loquacious. Thus the *Lycée* opened for me the long noon of French literature after Athens and Rome. And the sovereignty of the word.

Weekly, a sardonic classicist and student of Descartes came down from Yale to teach three of us – a Vichyite who was to turn into a modish painter, a Belgian anarchist, and myself – ancient

Greek. I carry still, under my right eye, the minute scar left by a sharp sliver of chalk which Monsieur B. hurled at me when I floundered over a passage in the wretched Athenian orator, Andocides. Latin was taught as the generator of French, as its ubiquitous font of perception and articulation. I was instructed that in literature as in art, originality signifies a return to origins (a lesson both true and laming if learned too early). These origins are philological and historical. The dictionary is a poet's breviary; a grammar is his missal, especially when he departs from it in heresy. In achieved form, be it in the poem, the sonata, or the painting, the past is made manifest presence, but without reneging or losing its historicity. It has been accorded "freedom of time," as we say of a man or a woman that they have been given the "freedom of the city." In what class-hour, from which harried or ironic or even faintly corrupt pedagogue, did I hear the quotation from Paul Eluard: *le dur désir de durer* ("the harsh, difficult desire to endure")? I believe that I knew on the instant that this would be my password. At the time, it meshed with my adoration for a student a year my senior. Of Russian origin, raven-haired, she had an elusive beauty heightened by nuances of disdain, particularly with regard to my moon-calf worship. Daylight and breath seemed to me to turn on her presence. That *dur désir.* Flattened by maturity, is one ever again so totally in love?

It was early spring. I recall precisely the chill, end-of-winter brightness over Central Park. News had filtered into the classroom of yet another atrocity. It was, I seem to remember, the large-scale, systematic hanging of hostages and civilians by the retreating Waffen-SS on the road north of Lyon. The air hung thick over our desks. With a hen's purposeful gait, in stomped the worn but occasionally inspired lady who taught modern French literature – where "modern" is defined as that written after 1600. She turned,

and has us turn, to Racine's *Bérénice*. We had, previously, analyzed
and committed to memory those lines from Antiochus' confession
of love to Bérénice which Madame ruled to be the apex of French,
which is simply to say, of Western literature:

> *Enfin, après un siège aussi cruel que lent,*
> *Il dompta les mutins, reste pâle et sanglant*
> *Des flammes, de la faim, des fureurs intestines,*
> *Et laissa leurs remparts cashés sous les ruines.*
> *Rome vous vit, Madame, arriver avec lui.*
> *Dans l'Orient désert quel devint mon ennui!*

We had been taught the magic of weight, the *rallentando* in that
opening, where *lent* makes "cruelty" heavier. Attention had been
drawn to those successive "f"-sounds in "flames," "famine," and
"fury," and to the lapidary concision and finality of ramparts buried under their own ruins. What mattered most was the ultimately
inexplicable wonder of the sixth verse, talismanic to the French
language and to French poetry after Racine: the understated infinity of desolation in the tension between the opulence of *Orient*
and the barrenness of *désert,* and that *ennui,* matchless in its
haughty despair. An entire realm has been made desert by one
absence. (Molière, also, makes a famously plangent, if ironic, resort to *désert* at the close of the *Misanthrope,* a usage that infuriated
the hermit in Rousseau.) It seemed to me that this bleak magic is
underwritten by the words immediately following: *Je demeurais
longtemps errant dans Césarée,* where *errant* conveys a dreary maze
of bewilderment, end-stopped by *Césarée,* a clarion-call invoking
the triumphant rival, Titus, Caesar-to-be.

Then, still under the dark of the day's news from France –
un siège aussi cruel que lent, by then four years of torture and

homicide – Madame took us to the close of the play. In a classic
the wholly familiar is also the unknown. Each recurrence is a first
home-coming. Bérénice's farewell to the competing monarchs, her
J'aimais, Seigneur: Je voulais être aimée, is like the clef of a civilization, of the way in which the life of a language determines the
resources of perception. In this adieu, formally of a Latin-Tacitean
sparseness, the tumult of the unspoken modulates into a lightness
of touch under supreme stress, uniquely Racine's. The senten-
tiousness, so Latin in its register of *Je l'aime, je le fuis; Titus m'aime,
il me quitte* – note how the rhyme on *conduite/quitte* crystallizes
the situation – now opens out, as into a twilit void: *De l'amour la
plus tendre et la plus malheureuse/puisse garder l'histoire douloureuse.*
In Racine's syntax, "love" is still feminine, a key instance of the
informing reciprocities between grammar and vision.

What can melt in a sexually ignorant, self-important fifteen-
year-old did so. The school-room, with its everyday odors of
cleaning-wax and spilled ink, blurred. A fear at the center took
hold of me; also an obscure hope. It became prescriptive in my
existence. I sensed, indistinctly, of course, that what I would, that
what I could know, taste, even smell of death before the fact would
be the moment of parting from the loved one, of a terror different
from, but no less lacerating than that of the abominations reported from across the sea; would be the last word, touch, or
glance exchanged between two human beings totally in love, possessed by the certitude that their sole chance of happiness would
lie in staying together. Bérénice's *Pour la dernière fois, adieu, Seigneur* gave me my first and lasting grasp of the tenor of death.
Where such an adieu has been anticipated, dreaded, and undergone, to the pitch of the unbearable, biological death is an after-
thought. Think, on a minor but comparable key, of the last time
one looks into the eyes of one's dog when taking him to the vet to

be put down. Titus' *Hélas!*, on which the curtain falls, marks the zero-hour of being. "Last time" has a total connotation. For the lovers, time itself ceases or enters the vacant fixity of midnight.

One other play, alert to *Bérénice*, fully enacts this extinction. It is Claudel's *Partage de midi*, when Ysé and Mésa exchange farewells in the last act. As in Racine, the parting of lover from beloved, of a man and a woman conjoined at the meridian of their identities, spells out the death before death. It conjures up the theology of irrecusable sorrow, of the soul in pain, which seems to inhabit the inmost of creation. That day, in the *Lycée*, there settled in me the intuition, juvenile but steadfast, that I would, in future, have to experience this *moment funeste*. Simultaneously, however, I experienced an uneasy hope. I hoped that I would come to know an act and season of love so complete, a rendezvous of body and spirit so encompassing of the meaning of life, that *pour la dernière fois* would, indeed, "put out the light, and then put out the light." Othello's doubling points first to the actual lamp, then to Desdemona's dying breath. But a larger definition beats within it. It is that of the first death, of that goodbye to the loved one, after which all other death is secondary. And, it may be, a relief.

I refer intentionally to *Othello*. Of men and women on record, Shakespeare had the uttermost capacity to speak the world. In him, so far as we can imagine, the synapses of language reticulated, entered into immediacies and energies of interaction and construction out of the ordinary. Both body and psyche, sensation and conception, must have taken on a linguistic cast at the threshold of consciousness or, in some manner, just prior to it, bringing to bear on intended meanings, on metaphor and image, pressures of possibility of exceptional strength. It was as if Shakespeare's inward and performative enlistment of words could harness not only their etymology and previous history, but the ambient and inter-

connecting potentialities of denotation and connotation, of phonetic associations as yet unexplored and of reserves latent in the
treasure-trove of the inchoate. Like no other "language-animal"
Shakespeare drew the sum of psychological and material reality,
the "things" which are our world, into an internet of word and
syntax. Special languages – legal, military, commercial, courtly,
theatrical, erotic, political, argotic – contribute to a fabric capable
of interrelating myriad aspects and a commonwealth of context to
the changing vitality of human affairs. In Shakespearian speech-
acts, root and branch are in dynamic interplay.

To this a further genius attaches. Shakespeare must have heard
any verbal fact, even within himself, immediately voiced. The
incipience of speech came with a speaker. This dramatization is
palpable even in the most private of the *Sonnets*. No concept,
however abstruse or finely labored, no proposition, however general and anonymous, seems to have come to him voiceless. It
arrived incarnate. *Per* usual, Shakespeare's own identification of
this advent is incomparable: it is "a bodying forth," it is the condensation of the universal into "a local habitation and a name." That of
the *dramatis persona,* either individual or polyphonic and choral.
Conceptual thought, argument, observation had for Shakespeare
the executive guise of action. He heard the pulse of existence as few
other men and women have, and was able to translate this "background noise" (the phrase used by current cosmology) into public
idiom. Hence the almost uncanny, inexplicable logic of feeling
which connects even his most singular, pathological, or transient
characters – a Feste, an Iago, a Trinculo – to the intelligible centers
of our humanity. A Shakespeare text remains defiant of summation
or complete diagnosis. It is perpetually new to the touch of production, performance, edition, or criticism. The English language has
become planetary in its wake.

These are banalities.

The consequence has been that there is very little "criticism" of Shakespeare, in any corrective or monitory sense of the word, after Samuel Johnson and Pope. To these Augustans, Shakespeare was a pre-eminent playwright often uneven in achievement, often technically awkward and of uncertain taste. Following on English and European romanticism, no such tranquillity of view is available. "Bardolatry," the self-projections of generations onto a persona such as Hamlet, rendered Shakespeare god-like. Passages from his plays are compared with the sublimities in the Gospels, not invariably to the latter's advantage. The works are proclaimed a shrine for mankind.

Dissents are few (but fascinating). Perhaps incensed by the eerie ways in which *King Lear* had acted out his own destiny and bitter nightfall before him, Tolstoy turned almost blindly on Shakespeare. He found him puerile, gross, insensitive to the just claims of common sense and social need. Between Tolstoy's infuriated lines on the imbecility of Gloucester's pretended leap from the Dover cliffs, we can discern a disturbing, poignant motif. Himself a playwright of considerable stature, Tolstoy felt repugnance at the humiliations of hysterical make-believe which such a scene inflicts on both actors and public. Shaw's giggly strictures, his pedagogic rewriting of *Cymbeline*, pertain to the sphere of pamphleteering fun and self-advertisement. A passing observation, on the other hand, by the young Lukács, subtlest of Marxist readers, arrests attention. There is, affirms Lukács, more political and historical understanding in Dante's *Paradiso* than in the entirety of William Shakespeare.

But it is Wittgenstein's marginalia which probably cut deepest. He can "make nothing of Shakespeare." He regards as suspect the consensus of adulation which haloes Shakespeare's *oeuvre*.

Such clamorous unanimity signals error. Wittgenstein can find in the plays no authentic truth to life. Real life, says Wittgenstein, is simply not "like that." Shakespeare is, no doubt, a supreme word-spinner. His characters, however, are solely aggregates of this semantic virtuosity. What is on display is a dazzling linguistic surface. Wittgenstein hammers home a point made, with characteristically feline discretion, by T. S. Eliot, when preferring Dante to Shakespeare. We can harvest from the utterances, from the conduct of Shakespeare's men or women no coherent ethics, no adult philosophy, let alone any enacted evidence of a transcendent faith. We know, says Wittgenstein, what is meant by "the great heart of Beethoven." No such finding applies to Shakespeare.

If we are aware of them at all, these rare detractions strike us as willfully erroneous. At best, they are psychological curios. They rattle like pebbles off the plinth of a treasured, indispensable colossus. How gray would be so many of our lives, so many of our languages without Shakespeare. It would be fatuous to emphasize that he never leaves me, that I have been privileged to "teach Shakespeare," whatever that locution may mean, throughout my profession. And yet.

Cornered, on some chat-show, into picking the one or two works of secular literature for that proverbial desert island, I would choose *Bérénice* and the *Commedia* (and cheat by binding in with *Bérénice* the *Partage de midi*). Shakespeare uses more than 20,000 different words; Racine a shade over 2,000. The difference is ontological. It declares two radically contrasting senses and sensings of the world. That of Shakespeare is prodigal, open-ended, and fluid as the stream of life itself; the other aims at essence through abstention. Racine is of the family of Bach's partitas, of Giacometti's figures, spare as the wind. He is a minimalist of immensity, aiming at indispensability in each touch. Remove a couplet from

Phèdre or *Bérénice,* and the tensed arch, the fugue of totally realized possibility, may collapse. Shakespeare is more often than not
performed incomplete. His purpose survives rearrangements and
merry or sinister follies of production. A play by Racine is a perfectly closed whole. One by Shakespeare is a script, brimful of
variant possibilities, open to transformative innovation, always
provisional. The images of man are almost antithetical.

Shakespearian presentments are begotten of that turbulent,
vulnerable, incessantly changing, pathetic, risible, and infinitely
moving substance which we call the human body. In Racine burns
the supposition that there are orders of moral and intellectual
clarity, of mortal *dignitas,* possible only when the body is forgotten, when the contingent, material world is excluded. No "roaring
hurricanoes," no woods on the march, no exits followed by bears.
A naked stage (only once, in Racine's *opus,* a chair, signifying utter
abdication). An empty space, an "anywhere" as featureless as Beckett's. A man and a woman, a woman and a man face one another.
Their speech is naked in its understatement. No noble or vile
corpses crowd the scene. Simply two adult human beings compelled to a terrible lucidity, to a truth of introspection and utterance which is, literally, fatal.

Shakespeare is tragi-comic in every fiber, as is our existence. He
knows that someone is being born next to or even on a lower floor
in the house of high death. That there is never only midnight or
noon. Fortinbras will prove to be an efficacious sovereign; Scot-
land will flower after Macbeth; Cyprus is certain to be better run
with excessive Othello gone. Even at the close of *Lear,* there is a
hint of consoling time. Racine imposes what Husserl called a
"bracketing," a setting aside of the natural, hybrid condition. In
an artifice of the absolute, Racine closes reality (Sartre's *No Exit*
can be read as a reflection on and of *Bérénice*). This closure, of

which the unities of time, place, and action are the formal executive mode, crystallizes the sum of being into one single instant,
into one collision – that of a man and woman at the plumbline of
parting. The word *univers* is the abolished counterpoint. "Let us
serve as example *à l'univers,*" urges Bérénice. The surrounding
universe has been brought to a stillness. It holds its breath as it
does in the narrative of present-day astrophysicists when they tell
of the inconceivably concentrated totality of force, of the "singularity" – a beautifully Racinian notion – outside normal time
and space in the nanoseconds before creation.

   This compaction empowers the unison of Racine's style. Shakespeare can be uneven, mixed, wasteful, inferior to himself, as is
human nature. Much in his bawdy is infantile. How many stag-
ings of *Othello* have included Desdemona's greasy banter with the
Clown? The demands of an open-air playhouse, of an audience
largely unfamiliar with the mythological-historical matter at
hand, required repetitive, top-heavy expositions (as, for example,
in *Hamlet*). Samuel Johnson ascribes to Shakespeare a native genius for comedy rather than tragedy. This may be so. But compare
the journeyman-work of *The Merry Wives of Windsor* to the mer-
curial sparkle and sadness of Verdi's *Falstaff.*

   Racine scarcely "passes" into English; nor does Claudel. *Macbeth,* I understand, is gripping in Swahili. To most literate English
speakers, my plea for the "essentiality" of *Bérénice* will seem bizarre. Thomas Otway's attempt at translation and importation in
1677 remains a forlorn one. Lifelong, I have tried to act as a
double or triple agent, seeking to suggest to one great language
and literature the necessary presence of the other. The craft of the
comparatist, of the translator is one of honest treason, of a persistent infidelity to any one tradition, culture, or community of
recognition. I have moved between tongues and contrasting ideals

of style, between literatures and educational systems. The inability to negotiate understanding and joy as between rival national-linguistic canons, the failure of import-export in so many vital cases, is never-ending. To how many in Britain or the United States are Corneille and Racine alive; who, in France, gauges the stature of George Eliot's *Middlemarch;* who save a clutch of poets and specialists outside German and Italian experience the gifts to our humanity made by Hölderlin and Leopardi? Am I mistaken in believing that, even in the light of Shakespeare, Dante's poetic intelligence and powers of organization remain unmatched?

This plurality of convictions across frontiers, this alleged absence from my writings of the somnambular innocence and authority of the native, monoglot spirit – the Cambridge shibboleth is *inwardness,* the German, *Blut und Boden,* the French, *la terre et les morts* – has provoked distaste, professional suspicion, and marginalization. A grateful wanderer, I have sought to press on my students and readers (the rewards were greatest in polyglot Geneva) that which is "other," which puts in doubt the primacy of household gods. What is now aching in me is the sense of doors unopened: my lack of Russian, for one, my lack of access to Islam, for another.

If I revert often to *Bérénice,* it is because, for me, that *coda* does enclose a universe. It is because it takes me back to the school day on which something of the centrality of love and of its inevitable contract with separation were brought home to me. As was the necessary menace which inhabits hope. The composition of the word adieu is no longer tangible in English. Indeed, when was it? In Bérénice's "last time," in the Pilgrim's farewell to Virgil in the *Purgatorio,* adieu speaks out, at the gates to silence, the word "God."

4

Only a Philip Roth could put into words the electricity, the blaze of every day at the University of Chicago in the late 1940s. Even the weather took on a theatrical grandeur. A south wind would choke the air with the red and stench of the meatyards. When, his hand broken, his eyes virtually sealed, Tony Zale won his title-fight by a somnambular knock-out of his Italian-American challenger, Zale's mates and backers in the White City steel-mills raised and then lowered the lights of their furnaces in tribute. I will never forget the sheen of jubilation, white-yellow and smoldering red, spreading across the lake. Or that August night on which, the temperature at sunset remaining still just above one hundred degrees Fahrenheit, the bull-horns of the campus police bellowed that we could leave our steaming dormitories (no air conditioning yet) and sleep in the park. Out we cascaded into the dark heat, the air a bit crazy with crickets and bolts of heat-lightning. Around us a city which never slept, whose brutal politics, art, jazz, classical music, atomic sciences, commerce, and racial tensions were palpable and charged to the touch. A megalopolis of pure intensity.

The two-tier bunks were jammed into dormitory cubicles overcrowded by returning veterans. The ex-paratrooper who was to be my room-mate stared at me in total disbelief. He had never laid eyes on a creature so obviously cosseted, sheltered, formally decked-out, book-laden, as I was. After a long, somehow raucous

silence, he asked me whether I was "smart." Gambling on survival,
I answered: "Phenomenally." He winced and wondered at the
word. He then inferred laconically that I might prove of some
servile use to him in getting through his courses, whose reading-
lists lay unkempt on the table. Now, however, he would show me
something I would *never* be able to match, not in a million years of
breathless trying. Alfie crouched on the floor, stretched both arms
in front of him in absolute tautness, and leapt into the upper
bunk. No Nureyev has surpassed for me the explosive arc of that
leap, displaying a paratrooper's perfect command over his tensed
thighs, over the hidden coil in the small of his back. I stood
transfixed, close to tears at my own awkwardness and the bare
beauty of that gesture. We agreed terms.

I would do my best to coach him in his academic tasks, to help
him towards the degree which the G.I. Bill of Rights had made
possible. He, in turn, would seek to make a passable human adult
of me, to teach me those arts of the ordinary which are for a book-
worm and privileged mandarin Jew the most arduous to acquire.
In the weeks following, I learned a little serious poker, I heard
Dizzy Gillespie's new jazz at the Beehive, I got over my fear of rats
and lavatories with broken cubicle-doors. Word went out. If, on
swarming 63rd Street or anywhere on that *louche,* racially simmer-
ing South Side, anyone so much as touched a hair on my swollen
head, they would have a paratrooper's karate-chop or knife to
reckon with. (Crouching on top of the urinal, Alfie had hawked
down on a rat and broken its spine with the flat of his hand.)
Wherever we went in that turbulent city, I walked next to or just in
front of my mentor like a baroque pilot-fish safe in the shadow of
his shark.

Memories of the flesh, especially sexual, have their own decep-
tive rhetoric. The actual episodes of trauma or epiphany are as

difficult to recapture, to articulate exactly as are shafts of pain. My
virginity offended Alfie. He found it ostentatious and vaguely
corrupt in a nineteen-year-old. He had made egalitarian love
against walls and under viaducts already as a boy. He sniffed the
fear in me with disdain. And marched me off to Cicero, Illinois, a
town justly ill famed but, by virtue of its name, reassuring to me.
There he organized, with casual authority, an initiation as thorough as it was gentle. It is this unlikely gentleness, the caring
under circumstances so outwardly crass, that blesses me still. As
does Alfie's sardonic but affectionately conspiratorial grin when we
returned to the edge of the Midway and he allowed me to treat
him to lobster and Caesar salad. He lifted me onto his gnarled
shoulders as we climbed back through our window into Burton-
Judson Court that night under a wind which hammered and sang
as it does only in Chicago. I have never inhaled that exact same
taste again, as of grain burning far away. In the shower, he
punched me hard. I was now "a man."

I wasn't, of course, not by a long shot. But a knot at the center
had been loosed, a fear made laughable. We chorused, off-tune, a
four-letter-word ditty out of the recent war. After which sleep,
even in that echoing dormitory heavy with disinfectant and tired
drains, was a celebration. It may sound absurd, but the enigma of
gentleness, the woman's patient humor (Alfie had briefed her)
brought to mind, to heart, Feste in *Twelfth Night:* "But when I
came to man's estate . . ." Wind and rain, as in Feste's lyrics, we
had in abundance. And those towering snows of the great plains
which remain the essence of America's monotonous majesty.
"Fucking won't kill you," ruled Alfie as he stood on his head letting
his stomach-muscles ripple. In which assurance he was, it may be,
only partly right. He got his B.A. The debt, however, was mine.

Having completed my French baccalaureat, I was admitted to

Yale on the understanding that the normal four-year undergraduate requirements could be shortened to two or two and a half. A
brief visit to Yale during "orientation week" made it plain to me
that Jews there were consigned to a ghetto of pinched politeness
(we are in 1949 and, unless I am mistaken, the very first Jew to
obtain tenure in the humanities had done so only the year before).
Providence – university terms had already begun – put in my way
an article on the University of Chicago and its legendary *condot-
tiere*. Scornful of the childish waste and banalities clogging American collegiate syllabi, Robert Maynard Hutchins allowed appli-
cants to sit examinations in almost every undergraduate discipline.
If they scored high enough, they were dispensed from taking the
relevant courses. This could, exceptionally, melt down the requi-
sites for a degree to one year. My performance in the sciences and
in sociology (even the word was new to me) was lamentable.
Coming out of the mandarinate of a French education with em-
phasis on Greek and Latin, I would, at Chicago, have four demanding terms ahead of me, taught by a number of the most
eminent physicists, chemists, biologists, and cultural anthropologists in the West.

Universities are, since their instauration in Bologna, Salerno, or
medieval Paris, fragile, although tenacious, beasts. Their place in
the body politic, in the ideological and fiscal power-structures of
the surrounding community, has never been unambiguous. The
fundamental tensions, furthermore, are inherent. No edifice, no
organization of higher learning has ever equilibrated satisfactorily
the competing claims of research, of specialized scholarship, of
bibliographic and archival conservation, with those of a general
education and civic training. Universities house diverse, often rival
parishes. The aims of the humanistic savant, of the speculative
thinker (to some degree solitary), of the scrutinizer of texts and

archives, of the remembrancer of an illustrious past, accord imperfectly, if at all, with the task of the pedagogue, of the general expositor. There is a recurrent sense, enshrined in the marmoreal hush of institutes for advanced study, in an All Souls at Oxford, in which the student is an intruder. This is, assuredly, so at the undergraduate level in the theoretical sciences. Ideally, major scholarship and philosophy *can* arise out of the business of teaching. I am persuaded that they should. Teaching and the companionship of mutual provocation in a seminar, have been my oxygen. I cannot imagine my work – even, to a vivid extent, my fiction – without them. If I struggle against retirement, it is because my students have been indispensable. This is good luck.

Paramount strengths in scientific research, on the other hand, in systematic investigation in the laboratory or at the algebraist's blackboard can be dazzling without comporting the vocation of the teacher. In certain respects, the springs of commitment are different, even contradictory (exceptions, such as Enrico Fermi at Chicago, become legend).

The dilemma does extend, however, also to the humanities. Both humanistic scholarship and scientific research have, or should have, their touch of monomania. They may communicate only haltingly the jealous fruit of an utter inwardness. Inevitably, there lurks in an effective, charismatic teacher an actor, a practitioner more or less acknowledged of locution and gesture. The scholastic persona, heir to a monastic-clerical code, retreats into the snail-house of its often esoteric labors. Pure truths can bear with anonymity. The great teacher is enmeshed, even bodily, with the communicative, exemplifying process. Arrestingly, abstruse metaphysical-logical inquiry and dialectic can, in the hands of an inspired teacher, become a memorable physique, a drama of mien and body. Socrates, Schelling, Wittgenstein, and Heidegger provide obvious instances.

These dissociations between research, scientific or humanistic, on the one hand, and teaching on the other, press on academe. How are institutions of tertiary education to combine – structurally, financially, sociologically – their custodianship of the historical-intellectual past with free innovation, with investment in the play, mainly scientific, of future possibility? And how is this uncertain dialectic to be aligned with the didactic syllabus, inevitably simplified, generalized, and socially-politically oriented? Neither the Thomist clerics of the early Sorbonne, nor Humboldt and his Berlin collaborators in the foundation of the modern university system, nor John Dewey have resolved contrarieties as old as the Athenian schools of rhetoric or the academies of Alexandria. I suspect that the future will bring about a widening gap between certain privileged centers of research and post-doctoral training and those colleges and universities devoted more explicitly to teaching. This may indeed prove unavoidable; but both enterprises will be losers.

The University of Chicago, during the late 1940s and the 1950s, may have come as close as any to housing the dynamic uncertainties, the collisions of purpose and *esprit* which characterize the notion, crazily arrogant and festive, of *universitas*. A special glow lay in that raw air.

A worthwhile university or college is quite simply one in which the student is brought into personal contact with, is made vulnerable to, the aura and the threat of the first-class. In the most direct sense, this is a matter of proximity, of sight and hearing. The institution, particularly in the humanities, should not be too large. The scholar, the significant teacher ought to be readily visible. We cross his or her daily path. The consequence, as in the Periclean *polis,* in medieval Bologna, or nineteenth-century Tübingen, is one of implosive and cumulative contamination. The whole is energized beyond its eminent parts. By unforced contiguity, the student, the young researcher, will (or should be) infected. He will catch the scent of the real thing. I resort to sensory terms because the impact can be physical. Thinkers, the erudite, mathematicians, or theoretical and natural scientists are beings possessed. They are in the grip of a mastering unreason.

What could, by the lights of the utilitarian or hedonistic commonwealth, be more irrational, more against the grain of common sense, than to devote one's existence to, say, the conservation and classification of archaic Chinese bronzes, to the solution of Fermat's last theorem, to the comparative syntax of Altaic languages (many now defunct), or to hairs-breadth nuances in modal logic? The requisite abstentions from distraction, the imperative labors, the tightening of nerve and brain to a constancy and pitch far beyond the ordinary, entail a pathological stress. The "mad professor" is the caricature, as ancient as Thales falling into the well, of a certain truth. There is something of a cancer, of autism in the necessary negations of common life, with its disheveled inconsequence and waste motion.

In the critical mass of a successful academic community, the orbits of individual obsessions will cross and re-cross. Once he has collided with them, the student will forget neither their luminosity nor their menace to complacency. This need not be (though it may be) a spur to imitation. The student may well come to reject the discipline in question, the ideology proposed. He or she may head, with relief, towards an altogether mundane, middling way of life. He or she may fail to take in the best of what is being taught or the philosophic-scientific debates around him or her. More

often than not, he or she may feel threatened by the mental powers, by the celebrity, be it hermetic or far-flung, of the masters
(e.g., that parking-space, at Berkeley, reserved for the exclusive use
of Nobel laureates). Almost unconsciously, excellence bullies.

No matter. Once a young man or woman has been exposed to
the virus of the absolute, once she or he has seen, heard, "smelt"
the fever in those who hunt after disinterested truth, something
of the afterglow will persist. For the remainder of their, perhaps,
quite normal, albeit undistinguished careers and private lives, such
men and women will be equipped with some safeguard against
emptiness.

The compaction, the density of encounter at Chicago was formidable. In my twelve months as an undergraduate, I was allowed
to hear Fermi introducing particle physics to students in the very
locale in which he had initiated the first controlled chain-reaction.
Harold Urey delivered a number of introductory lectures in chemistry. Aristotelian-Thomist epistemology modulated, with Richard McKeon, into the stormy politics of the day. Redfield taught
social anthropology; Allen Tate, poetics (I will come back to both
Tate and McKeon). Hence the osmotic pressure of interconnec-
tion which activated Hutchins's utopia of cultural coherence, of
universality in the medieval sense.

Provided they kept mute, undergraduates were allowed to sit in
advanced seminars. Enter Leo Strauss: "Ladies and gentlemen,
good morning. In this class-room, the name of . . . who is, of
course, strictly incomparable, will not be mentioned. We can now
proceed to Plato's *Republic.*" "Who is, of course, strictly incomparable." I had not caught the name, but that "of course" made me
feel as if a bright, cold shaft had passed through my spine. A kindly
graduate student wrote down the name for me at the close of the
class: one Martin Heidegger. I trotted to the library. That evening, I

attempted paragraph one of *Sein und Zeit*. I failed to grasp even the briefest, seemingly straightforward sentence. But the vortex was spinning, the irradicable intimation of a world new to me in depth. I vowed to try again. And again. This is the point. To direct a student's attention towards that which, at first, exceeds his grasp, but whose compelling stature and fascination will draw him after it. Simplification, leveling, watering down, as they now prevail in all but the most privileged education, are criminal. They condescend fatally to the capacities unbeknown within ourselves. Attacks on so-called elitism mask a vulgar condescension: towards all those judged *a priori* to be incapable of better things. Both thought (knowledge, *Wissenschaft*, imagination given form) and love ask too much of us. They humble us. But humiliation, even despair in the face of difficulty – one has sweated the night through and, still, the equation is unsolved, the Greek sentence not understood – can lighten at sun-up. In those two years at Chicago, one as an undergraduate, one in graduate-school, the mornings were prodigal.

Also the nights away from the desk. Along the lake-shore with its singular drumming, part traffic in the sleepless city, part those great winds which, even becalmed, seemed to inhabit the slate waters. Nights at parties thick with smoke and politics and probably, though I did not realize it, with early, fairly bucolic drug-taking. The populist left of Henry Wallace had pitched its tents on the campus. There were self-styled, but also initiated, communists home from the wars, who had read little Marx and less Hegel but intoned mournful ballads out of Catalonia, the Lincoln Brigade, and the slave-culture of the deep South. Their wives produced memorable pastrami sandwiches on Jewish rye. Trotskyites had their own covens and longed for Mexico. There was a fistful of black activists from the trade-union movement, mature students inspired by a sort of angry innocence (one of them was later gunned down by the trucker's mafia in a jurisdictional shoot-out in Omaha). And all around these heroics and this utopian impatience, a buzz of young, not so young women, on the fringe of the University. With one of these, neurotic to her cigarette-stained fingertips, I believed myself to be in love. She was charitably amused.

Examinations were in the offing. In one of the American literature courses, the set texts included Henry James's *The Golden Bowl*. This novel is a somewhat overwrought, involuted parable which a number of the inmates in my dormitory found intractable. Could I help? I thought I could, and roughly a dozen of us gathered in the kitchen of one of the housing developments for veterans and married students off 63rd Street. Had they, among other points, noticed that the name of one of the characters, Fanny Assingham, conflated, grossly, improbably in the midst of that Jamesian *petit-point* and obliquity, three designations of the posterior? I will never forget the swoop of silence in the room, the awe on the faces of men so much more adult, so much better acquainted with life than I was.

Not long after, a group came to my room. They crowded the upper and lower bunks and the floor. Could I be of use in regard to Joyce's story, "The Dead"? There are few short fictions more manifold, more interleaved with pressures of remembered history and the gradual revelation of intent. Few in which it would be impossible to omit a sentence without impairing the intelligence, the commanding shape of the whole. I found myself conducting an unauthorized seminar into the long night, reading with and just ahead of these concentrated listeners. I glimpsed them taking notes, underlining and filling the margins in their text. I spoke of the sheer musicality of the story. Songs and song-titles are as informing in "The Dead" as they are in *Twelfth Night* or *Finnegans Wake*. I read aloud the finale:

> Yes, the newspapers were right: snow was general all over Ireland. It was falling on every part of the dark central plain, on the treeless hills, falling softly upon the Bog of Allen and, further westward, softly falling into the dark mutinous Shannon waves. It was falling, too, upon every part of the lonely churchyard on the hill where Michael Fury lay buried. It lay thickly drifted on the crooked crosses and headstones, on the spears of the little gate, on the barren thorns. His soul swooned slowly as he heard the snow falling faintly through the universe and faintly falling, like the descent of their last end, upon all the living and the dead.

Had they observed the ancient rhetorical figure (the Greek name for it was . . .) whereby "falling softly" modulates into "softly falling" so as to prelude the motion from "falling faintly" to "faintly falling"? Or the sibilants of nearing slumber in that "soul swooning slowly"? Worth underlining were those "spears" and "thorns," emblematic of Christ's passion on another hill, long ago. But the hour had grown late and the air in the room was stale. I tried to block absurd tears. Until I saw them on some of those unshaved faces. I knew now that I could invite others into meaning. It was a fateful discovery. From that night on, the Sirens of teaching and interpretation sang for me.

5

To a sliver of land, without oil; amid a population far below that of many a modern metropolis – came the representatives
of 131 nations. Thrones, Dominions, Powers, the crowned heads,
potentates, heads of state, pontiffs, prime ministers, gangsters of
the planet assembling at the funeral of Yitzhak Rabin. Some in
grief or sympathy, some in unctuous indifference or opportunism,
more than a clutch in concealed satisfaction and hatred. But they
came. From every corner of the earth, as they would have to no
other pomp. *Of course there is a Jewish question.* Only cant or a self-
deluding investment in normalcy could deny that. The political
map, the plethora of ethnic-historical legacies, the patchwork of
societies, faiths, communal identifications across our globe teems
with unresolved conflicts, with religious-racial enmities, with non-
negotiable claims to an empowering past, to sacred grounds.
Nonetheless, the Jewish condition differs. Irreducibly, madden-
ingly, it embodies what modern physics calls a "singularity," a
construct or happening outside the norms, extraterritorial to prob-
ability and the findings of common reason. Judaism pulses and
radiates energy like some black hole in the historical galaxy. Its
parameters are those of "strangeness," another key-notion in current theoretical physics and cosmology.

Why have Jews survived?

The peoples of ancient Egypt and Sumeria were fruitful and in-
ventive. The example and achievements of ancient Greece, be they

in politics or science or art or philosophy, continue to animate Western culture. There has not been a civilization more effectively marshaled, more insistent on law than that of republican and imperial Rome. No direct descendants subsist of these eminent nations. Their languages are ghosts for the learned. The Jews exist; in Israel and the Diaspora. Hebrew is spoken, written, adapted to nuclear physics, dreamt in. After more than two millennia of systematic and fitful persecution, of scattering into exile, of suffocation in the ghetto, after the Holocaust. Jews insist on existing *contra* the norm and logic of history, which, even barring genocide, are those of gradual melting, assimilation, cross-breeding, and the effacement of original identity. They exist *contra* the voracious dictates and measures of tyrannies, hostile faiths, mass-movements such as the blood-mobs of medieval Christendom or the pogroms of eastern Europe and Russia. All these were explicitly launched to eliminate Jews from humankind. To make the air and the earth *Judenrein,* "Jew-cleansed" (an appetizing epithet which Hitler borrowed from earlier Austrian usage). To make of every Jewish man, woman, and child (also unborn) ash blown to the wind. Babylon, Thebes, Carthage are archaeology. Modern Athens is a travesty of an unredeemable past. The laws, the epigraphy of imperial Rome turn up in the desert. Israel relives; the Diaspora, notably in North America, is animate with creative force and a lust for renewal. Despite ostracism, pariahdom, massacre, and the perhaps fated – because of their theological source in certain founding principles of Christianity, in the exorcism of Judas – abomination of the gas-ovens. Despite the temptations of "passing" unnoticed into liberal modernity, of ebbing into normalcy and amnesia. Why?

For the Orthodox and the conservative believer, the answer is clarion-clear. God had promised Abraham that his seed would engender a people numerous as the stars, that Canaan would be his and his progeny's. The contract of election for survival is renewed with Moses. Be it for exceptional suffering or intimacy with the God of Abraham, Isaac and Jacob – where suffering and intimacy are as inseparable as voices in a dialogue – the Jew has been chosen and branded for eternity. If he was to perish from this earth, God's truth and declared intent, the revelation of monotheism and of morality on Sinai, would be falsified. So long as one man and one woman survive out of the house of Jacob, so long as they can bear children, which is one of the cardinal duties and joys in Judaism, God is still neighbor to man and to creation. Incommensurable as it is to human reason and imagining, unbearable as it must always be to recollection, Auschwitz is ephemeral as compared with the Covenant, with God's re-insurance of His hunted people. Hitler could no more prevail than could Nebuchadnezzar or the Inquisition. There were rabbis who exultantly proclaimed this axiom on the edge of the fire-pits.

How enviable are the undoubting.

Pragmatists, relativists, the skeptical spirits who regard overarching theories of history, especially when these are deterministic and teleological, as dangerous delusions, see no cause for special wonder or irrational causation. Certain practices of endogamy, of self-isolation in early Judaism, an adherence to archaic but therapeutic dietary precautions, the retention of a liturgical-legal code and language, explain the anomaly of survival. Even more important were the reflexes of coherence, of self-recognition provoked by the very pressures of ever-renewed hostility and persecution. Nor, argues the secularist, should one overstate continuity. Ethnically, the Jews are, like everyone else, a mixed lot. Perhaps a touch less mixed and more biosocially distinct than many other communal congeries (does "race" exist in any verifiable sense?), but hybrid nevertheless. The Jews' prolonged history, like that,

say, of the Chinese, results from a peculiar interplay of isolation
and external constraints. It is not some theological-ontological
mysterium. Demographic pointers, certainly in the liberal-secular
West, strongly suggest that assimilation and self-forgetfulness in a
climate of increasing tolerance or indifference may, at last, edge
the chronicle of Judaism to an anodyne close. Only certain Orthodox communities, even within a secularized Israel, will retain any
authentic, separate identity. Any other view, moreover, runs the
risk of sustaining racism and race-hatreds.

These are eminently plausible arguments. Would that I could
subscribe. Yet intuition tells me that the great narrative out of
Abraham, the story which the God of Sinai has been telling Himself, will not end in benign eclipse. First, a question, almost taboo.

Has the survival of the Jew been worth the appalling cost?
Would it not be preferable, on the balance-sheet of human mercies, if he was to ebb into assimilation and the common seas? It is
not only the horrors of our century, of the Hitlerite-Stalinist persecution and mass-murder of Jews which enforce the question. It is
not only the midnight of man at Auschwitz. It is the aggregate of
suffering since, say, the destruction of Jerusalem and the second
Temple in A.D. 70. It is the unending homicide, humiliation,
pariahdom visited on Jewish men, women, and children nearly
every day, nearly every hour, in some quarter of the "civilized"
world. As consuming – the long history of flame climaxing in the
Shoah – as the actual violence, has been the fear, the degradation,
the miasma of contempt, latent or explicit, which has stained
Jewish lives in gentile streets, institutions, and courts of law (Shy-
lock on his knees). What Jewish child, across the millennia, has
not known the gamut of threats and derision, of exclusion or
condescension which extends from blows, stones thrown, from
being spat on, all the way to the urbane distaste, to the welcome

"on sufferance" offered by the gentile? Every Jewish father is, at some point in his life and paternity, an Abraham to an Isaac on that unspeakable three-day journey to Mount Moriah. Genesis 22 is at the bruised heart of all Judaism. When he begets a child, a Jew knows that he may be bestowing on that child the inheritance of terror, of a sadistic destiny. Long before the Holocaust, spurts of genocide (the medieval massacres in the Rhineland, the tracking down of recusant Jews by the Inquisition, the pogroms in the east) aimed to eradicate the Jew. Not, in any final analysis, on religious, political, economic, or social grounds – though these played their part. The purpose, honestly stated by Nazism, was ontological. It was the wiping from this earth of Jewish being. The unborn had to be murdered. The non-negotiable guilt of the Jew was that of existence. Having engendered his child, a Jewish father, across Russia and Europe, in the streets of Hebron or near a Paris synagogue, has made that child guilty. For a Jew to be has, in the eyes of the haters, been original sin.

Furthermore, and this is a crux (ominous word) often overlooked, victimization, ostracism, torture are dialectic. They knit both parties to each other. Hunter and hunted are bound obscenely close. Over the centuries, anti-Semitism – a somewhat absurd term, as it flourishes within Islam – has demeaned its perpetrators. In the death-camps, man, as a species, lowered, permanently perhaps, the precarious threshold of his humanity. He stepped backward into the bestial, though to phrase it this way is to insult the primate and animal worlds. In dehumanizing his or her victim, the butcher dehumanizes himself or herself. The stench endures. There have been other persecutions, enslavements, and killing-fields. Tribal massacres continue. But these have not persisted against any one group over 2,000 years. Often, they have been avenged. It is the hideous one-sidedness of the Jewish circumstance, until 1948 and

Israel, which has, time and again, led other faiths and societies into the seductions of the inhuman. What I am asking is this: might the Christian West and Islam live more humanely, more at ease with themselves, if the Jewish problem were indeed "resolved" (that *Endlösung* or "final solution")? Would the sum of obsessive hatred, of pain, in Europe, in the Middle East, tomorrow, it may be, in Argentina or South Africa, be diminished? Is liberal erosion, is intermarriage the true road? I do not think the question can simply be shrugged aside.

Yet how disproportionately radiant has been the Jewish contribution. That of the Hebrew Bible and of the ethics which burgeon from it is incommensurable. For better or for worse, Rome and Mecca are the daughters (matricidal?) of Jerusalem. Consider only modernity and the climate of our age. Cliché has it that this climate stems directly from Marx, Freud, and Einstein (though Darwin must, surely, be added). More than a hundred tongues characterize their bureaucracies, the gray anonymities, the neuroses of their social fabric by the name (usually made an adjective!) of Franz Kafka. The count of illustrious scientists, those visitors to Stockholm, who are Jews, at least in origin, is so above any statistical norm or expectation as to be gloriously embarrassing. Music has been provoked to radical rebirth by Schoenberg; anthropology by Lévi-Strauss; philosophy by Wittgenstein; economic theory by Kenneth Arrow. It is by the light of Proust that we descend the spiral staircase into the self (an image devised by the half-Jew, Montaigne). Any catalogue would be interminable and otiose.

What is more difficult to articulate is the extent to which modernity *per se,* notably in the exemplary and dominant American vein, is so markedly "Jewish." To a graphic extent, the mass-media, the humor, the fiscal and mercantile sinews of global enterprise which now threaten to homogenize the globe, are energies, vast arcs of electrifying shock, which have sprung out of emancipated Judaism. I have watched oriental audiences helpless with laughter, grasping instantaneously the wholly Jewish, dare one say "Talmudic," anti-rhetoric and black humor of a Woody Allen film. Supermarkets, invented and first stylized by a Jew in Washington during the Second World War, are now opening in Albania. But even these universals, near to uncanny in a matrix of survivors, are, in some sense, of the surface.

Could our lamed civilizations dispense with the Jewish ideal of the family? It is these which derived from and, in turn, underwrite the unique Jewish "familiarity" with God, the "familial" values which fuel the Jew's never-ending colloquy with God even, one suspects, on the silent lips of the agnostic. Is there any other tribe so *krank an Gott* – Karl Barth's magnificently untranslatable designation of the Jew as "God-sick," as "afflicted with/by God"? Which infirmity may entail man's survival as a moral being still "vulnerable to the wounds of negativity" (Kierkegaard). In brief: even if a "passing-out" seems to offer Jews in the Diaspora the prospect of release from offense and peril, even if secular Jews were to decide that the price of continued identity is no longer worth paying – what of their reluctant hosts? Can Western history and culture do without its Jews? As Heine, that most caustic of Jewish self-ironists opined, even pure-bred dogs do need their fleas.

Alas, I cannot feel myself a party to a contract with Abraham. Thus I am no owner of a freehold, divinely countersigned, on some acre in the Middle-East – or anywhere else. It is the logical flaw in Zionism, a secular-political movement, to invoke a theological-scriptural mystique to which it cannot, in avowed truth, subscribe. Nonetheless, the enigma, the singularity of the survival of the Jew after the Shoah, persuades me of a purpose. Israel is an *indispensable miracle*. Its coming into being, its persistence against military,

geopolitical odds, its civic achievements, defy reasoned expectation. Today it looks with paradoxical satisfaction to normalcy: to
the dosages of crime, corruption, political mediocrity, and vul-
garities of the everyday which characterize nations and societies
everywhere. Where Jeremiah thundered, there are topless bars.

This, precisely, is where I balk. It would, I sense, be somehow
scandalous (a word with a theological provenance) if the millennia
of revelation, of summons to suffering, if the agony of Abraham
and of Isaac, from Mount Moriah to Auschwitz, had as its last
consequence the establishment of a nation-state, armed to the
teeth, a land for the bourse and the mafiosi, as are all other lands.
"Normalcy" would, for the Jew, be just another mode of disap-
pearance. The riddle, perhaps the madness, of survival must have a
greater calling. One that is integral to exile.

All of us are guests of life. No human being knows the meaning
of its creation, except in the most primitive, biological regard. No
man or woman knows the purpose, if any, the possible significance
of its "thrownness" into the mystery of existence. Why is there not
nothing? Why am I? We are guests of this small planet, of an
infinitely complex, perhaps chancy weave of evolutionary processes and mutations which, at innumerable points, might have
gone otherwise or witnessed our extinction. As it has turned out,
we are vandal-guests, laying waste, exploiting and destroying other
species and resources. We are rapidly turning to poisonous garbage
this uncannily beautiful, intricately adjusted environment, and
even outer space. There are trash-bins on the moon. Inspired as it
is, the ecological movement which, together with a nascent perception of the rights of children and of animals, is among the few
lit chapters in our century, may have come too late.

Yet even the vandal is a guest, in a house of being he has not built and whose design, in all connotations of that term, escapes him. Now we must learn to be one another's guests on what remains of this scarred, crowded earth. Our wars, our ethnic cleansings, the arsenals for massacre which flourish in even the most destitute of states, are territorial. Ideologies and the mutual hatreds they generate are territories of the mind. Men have, from the outset, slaughtered one another over a patch of ground, under differently colored rags held aloft as banners, over shadings of difference in language or dialect. Hamlet wonders at a passing army. Why is it marching to bloody battle? Is it to gain some exalted or fruitful end? A captain answers:

> Truly to speak, and with no addition,
> We go to gain a little patch of ground
> That hath in it no profit but the name.
> To pay five ducats, five, I would not farm it;
> Nor will it yield to Norway or the Pole
> A ranker rate should it be sold in fee.

History has seen the unending application of reciprocal loathing to motives often trivial and irrational. At a lunatic spark, communities, such as in the Balkans or throughout Africa, after having lived together over centuries or decades, can explode into apartheid and genocide. Trees have roots, men and women have legs. With which to traverse the barbed-wire idiocy of frontiers, with which to visit, to dwell among the rest of mankind as guests. There is a fundamental implication to the legends, numerous in the Bible, but also in Greek and other mythologies, of the stranger at the door, of the visitor who knocks at the gate at sundown after his or her journey. In fables, this knock is often that of a concealed god or divine emissary testing our welcome. I would want to think of these visitors as the truly *human* beings we must try to become if we are to survive at all.

It may be that the Jew in the Diaspora survives in order to be a guest – so terribly unwelcome still at so many shut doors. Intrusion may be our calling, so as to suggest to our fellow men and women at large that all human beings must learn how to live as each other's "guests-in-life." There is no society, no region, no city, no village not worth improving. By the same token, there is none not worth leaving when injustice or barbarism take charge. Morality must always have its bags packed. This has been the universalist precept of the prophets, of Isaiah, Deutero-Isaiah, and Jeremiah in their ancient quarrel with the kings and priests of the fixed nation, of the fortress-state. Today, this polemic underlies the tensions between Israel and the Diaspora. Though the thought must, like the ritual name of God, be unspeakable, the greater verity is that Judaism would survive the ruin of the state of Israel. It would do so if its "election" is indeed one of wandering, of the teaching of welcome among men, without which we shall extinguish ourselves on this minor planet. Concepts, ideas, which exceed in strength any weapons, any *imperium,* need no passports. It is hatred and fear which issue or deny visas. I have felt more or less at home – the Jew is often a polyglot almost unawares – wherever I have been allowed a table to work at. *Nihil alienum,* said the Roman playwright. "Nothing human is alien to me." Or to put it another way: what other human presence can be stranger to myself than, at times, I am?

Is it this unhousedness and intuition of the peregrine which foster anti-Semitism, which nourish the image of the Jew's opportunistic infidelities? Stalin and Hitler made of the glorious noun "cosmopolitan," with its promise of the inalienable, a murderous sneer. But did not Rashi himself, acutest of Talmudic readers, tell of the everlasting need for Abraham to abandon his tent and rejoin the road? Did Rashi not instruct us that, when asking the way, a Jew should prove deaf to the right answer, that his mission lay with being errant, which is to say, in error and wandering?

Undoubtedly, this commitment to transience, even where it is imposed, this companionship with the winds, inspires a visceral distrust. The Nazi term was *Luftmensch*, creatures of the air, rootless (and thus to be made ash). It compounds other elements in the long tale of Jewish leprosy. There are social factors, economic jealousies, the instinctual search for the scapegoat, circumcision, the obduracy of apartness. Walled-in, ghetto-Judaism had entered on a contract of strangeness, of "otherness" with its gentile despisers. All these go into the venomous brew of difference and persecution. Yet, no serious aspect of the Jewish problem, of the history and life of the Jew, can ever be divorced altogether from theological-metaphysical sources (how often I heard Gershom Scholem hammer at this nerve). It is, in the final analysis, the theological and the metaphysical which inform the tragic complication of the facts.

I have, throughout my work, and most explicitly in *In Bluebeard's Castle* (1971), argued that it is not the accusation of deicide, of the alleged complicity of the Jews in the killing of Jesus of Nazareth, which underlies and sustains Western anti-Semitism. No doubt, Jew-hatred is formidably augmented by Pauline Christianity and the Church Fathers. But it predates these fatalities. I believe that it is not the "slaying of God in the person of his son" – whatever that macabre phantasm is taken to signify – which is fundamental to the detestation of the Jew. It is the narrative "creation," "invention," "definition," "revaluation" of God in Jewish monotheism and its ethics. It is not as killer but as "begetter" of God that the Jew is unforgiven.

Three times, in Western history, the Jew has striven to confront human consciousness with the concept of the one God and the moral-normative consequences of that concept. Rigorously apprehended, the Mosaic God is inconceivable, incomprehensible, invisible, unattainable, in-human in the root-sense of the word. He is blank as the desert air. If there is a Jewish theology, it is negative. Where polytheism, particularly Hellenic, crowds every leaf and branch and rock with divine neighbors, prodigally immanent, human – all too human in their vanities, tricks, lubricities – Sinai empties of any discernible divine proximity the habitat of natural man. It demands an extremity of abstraction. It condemns images and makes a blasphemy of imagining. Metaphor, whereby we people and dramatize our questioning of reality, whereby we throw bridges across the abyss of the unknown, is cut off.

To Moses, God's presence and commandment, which are identical, burn out of the Bush. The sole self-disclosure is that of a tautology (itself a closed figure): it is the "I Am/I Am" of Exodus 3:14. Paradoxically, however, the distance to an imageless, unthinkable, unsayable God is also that of an unbearable nearness. Unseen, He sees all, He chastises to the third generation and beyond. Can there be a harsher observing and observance, one more alien to the animistic, iconic, pluralistic impulses of human nature, to the consoling ways in which we tell the stories of our being?

The moral dictates which emanate from Sinaitic and prophetic monotheism are uncompromising. Prohibitions on murder, on adultery, on greed, on the making of images, however innocent, on commerce with house-gods, tutelary spirits, saints, are themselves symptoms of a deeper demand. They entail the mutation of common man. We are to discipline soul and flesh into perfection. We are to outgrow our own shadow. A fundamental edict of ethical self-fulfillment, of self-surpassing, underwrites the Decalogue and the plethora of ritual-pragmatic prescriptions that follows. No fiber of our native complaisance, libido, inattention, mediocrity, and sensualities escapes moral and legalistic exposure. Taken *à la lettre,* Nietzsche's "become what you are" is the antithesis to the Sinai-imperative. "Cease being what you are, what biology and circumstance have made you. Become, at a fearful price of abnegation, what you could be." So ordains the God of Moses, of Amos, of Jeremiah.

This is the first of the three moments of transcendent imposition on man out of Judaism.

The second comes with the Sermon on the Mount. Most of the message is a collage of thoroughly rehearsed injunctions from the Torah, the psalms, and the Prophets. But the wonder-rabbi and faith-healer from Galilee goes further. He requires of men and of women an altruism, a counter-instinctual, "unnatural" restraint towards all who do us injury and offense. The only precedent for this ideal may be read between the lines of some pronouncements, difficult to interpret, attributed to Socrates. We are, moreover, to share or give away altogether our worldly possessions, to beggar ourselves, if need be, on behalf of the destitute. Possessions, let alone mundane rewards, are injustice (or as Proudhon was to put it, "theft"). These are quantum leaps from within, but also beyond Mosaic Judaism. Nearly inconceivably against the human grain is Jesus' bidding that we offer the other cheek, that we forgive our enemy and persecutor – no, that we learn to *love* him. With these requirements, Jesus becomes Christ and amends elemental instincts, notably that of vengeance, in his own Jewishness. God's

infinite mercy and powers of forgiveness are expounded in the
Torah and prophecies, but so is His taste for the grim equities of
retribution. The profoundly natural impulse to avenge injustice,
oppression, and derision do have their place in the house of Israel.
A refusal to forget injury or humiliation can warm the heart.
Christ's ordinance of total love, of self-offering to the assailant, is,
in any strict sense, an enormity. The victim is to love his butcher.
A monstrous proposition. But one shedding fathomless light.
How are mortal men and women to fulfill it?

The third knock at the door is that of utopian socialism, notably in its Marxist guise. Together with Christianity, Marxism is
Judaism's other principal heresy. The Jewish theoretical, practical,
and personal contribution to radical socialism and pre-Stalinist
communism is out of all proportion (cf. the manning of the early
Mensheviks and Bolsheviks or of the left-wing utopian and insur-
rectionary movements throughout central Europe). Marxism sec-
ularizes, makes "of this world" the messianic logic of social justice,
of Edenic plenty for all, of peace on an undivided earth. In his
famous manuscript-notes of the 1840s, Marx, so rabbinic in thun-
der and promise, preaches an order in which the currency will no
longer be that of lucre and goods: "love shall be exchanged for
love, trust for trust." It is, literally, the vision of the Adamic and of
the prophets; it is that of the Galilean. The great rage against social
inequality, against the sterile cruelty of wealth, against unnecessary
famine and *misère* which goads Karl Marx is precisely that of
Amos. It is that of the desert on its avenging march against the
city, against the continuing Babylon. (There was, in the blood-
madness of the Khmer Rouge in Cambodia, more than a touch of
that apocalyptic reckoning.)

In its purest form, as enacted in certain socialist-communist
Kibbutzim in early Zionism, there is no private property. To each

according to his needs. Children are cared for communally. But even where it attenuates such absolutes, Marxism demands a complete inversion of the priorities of privacy, of acquisition, of egoism. We are to abstain from superfluity, to share and share alike, to invest the resources, the ambitions of the self in the anonymity of the collective. At the core of any consistent socialist-communist program lies a mystique of altruism, of a human ripening into unselfishness. To die for others, as does the Marxist hero in secular figurations of religious martyrdom, is difficult enough (who, of my generation, can forge the closing episodes of sacrifice in Malraux's *Condition humaine?*). To live for others is even harder. But only if we learn to do so, enjoins Marxism, can the kingdom of justice, can the city of man – legitimate heir to that of a dead God – be built on this earth. Only then can Jerusalem be built "in our green and pleasant lands." The messianic morning is red.

Three times, Judaism has brought Western civilization face to face with the blackmail of the ideal. What graver affront? Three times, like a crazed watcher in the night (Freud has even woken men from innocent dreaming), it has cried out to common humankind to transform itself into full humanity, to renege its ego, its inborn appetites, its bias to license and options. In the name of the "unspeakable" God on Sinai; of love unbounded for one's enemy; at the behest of social justice and economic equality. In their claims to perfection, these demands are irrefutable. The ethic of sacrificial love and sharing is unanswerable; even, at many points, on a material-communal level. Thus there has been a threefold blackmail pressed on men and women with the tactlessness of revelation, with that Jewish intensity and insinuation which non-Jews often find it so hard to live with. The ideal of Moses, Jesus, and Marx hammer at the psyche of *l'homme moyen sensuel,* seeking to get on with his imperfect existence.

Of this pressure, I believe, is loathing bred. From it smolders
and bursts into flame the impulse of relegation – the Jew must be
banished, his voice gagged – and then of annihilation. Nothing
fuels a deeper hatred in our consciousness than the insight, forced
on us, that we are falling short, that we are betraying ideals whose
validity we fully (even if subliminally) acknowledge, indeed celebrate, but whose requirements seem to lie beyond our capacities or
will. Nothing grows more unbearable than to be reminded recurrently, perpetually it would seem, of what we ought to be and, so
crassly, are not. Today, coercive utopian socialism and communism appear to be fading; the Sparta of the absolute Kibbutz
hardly survives. But still the ancient dictates of perfection, of self-
annulment, the exigence of a kingdom of total justice here and
now, can be heard. Out of the mouths of despised wanderers, of
loquacious vagrants whom God has made incurably sick with
remembrance and futurity.

I confess to finding no better explanation for the persistence of
anti-Semitism more or less world-wide and after the Holcaust.
This persistence is exemplary in communities where there are
scarcely any Jews left to detest, such as Poland or Austria, or where
they have never even settled (the so-called *Protocols of Zion* are a
best-seller in Japan!). No positivist socio-economic-political diag-
noses, however illuminating, provide any causation in depth. Hitler put it bluntly: "The Jew has invented conscience." After that,
what forgiveness?

I have said that the price paid has been near to unendurable.
That there is a sane argument for effacement into assimilation and
normalcy. If some repetition of or analogy to the Shoah is conceivable in the future, ought a Jew to bring children into this world?
Neverthelesss.

The vocation of the "guest," the aspiration to the messianic, the function of the moral irritant and insomniac among men, does strike me as an honor beyond honors. Wherever, whenever they are present or prosper, bestiality, stupidity, intolerance will choose the Jew for their target. Truly, a chosen people and a club I would not resign from (even if this was feasible). There is a work-sheet:

Man will make it his purpose to master his own feelings, to raise his instincts to the heights of consciousness, to make them transparent, to extend the wires of his will into hidden recesses and thereby raise himself to a new plane . . .

Man will become immeasurably stronger, wiser and subtler; his body will become more harmonized, his movements more rhythmic, his voice more musical. The forms of life will become dynamically dramatic. The average human type will rise to the heights of an Aristotle, a Goethe, or a Marx. And above this ridge new peaks will rise.

Author: one Lev Davidovitch Bronstein (also known as Trotsky). A text written in the heat of battles as fierce as Joshua's. Nonsense, isn't it? But nonsense to live and to die by.

6

There are sentences which arrest the spirit. They map spaces we traverse, re-traverse, seek to quarry, and inhabit. Take the proposition by Hans Keller (acerbic critic and musicologist): "As for Beethoven, possibly humanity's greatest mind altogether . . ." Set beside it the notation in Adorno's incomplete, posthumous *Beethoven*: "Hitler and the IX. Symphony. *Seit umzingelt Millionen*" ("Be surrounded, be conjoined in embrace, ye millions"). Triangulate these two remarks with Claude Lévi-Strauss's dictum: "invention of melody: supreme mystery in *les sciences de l'homme*" – in the sciences, in the body of rational thought and information bearing on mankind. Sentences that stake out a terrain for life-long exploration and questioning.

They refer to music, they predicate judgments on music. Whatever their musicological authority and suggestion, they remain irreparably linguistic, verbal. Three domains, that of the nature and nomination of God, that of higher mathematics and that of music (how are these interrelated?) set the boundary conditions of language. They delimit the outermost reaches and constraints of lexical-grammatical discourse. But these boundaries are, as it were, active. There are vital truths and illuminations in their demonstration of the inaccessible. They instruct us, as do the seeming paradoxes of relativity theory, that language is, within itself, infinite, that it is incommensurable in its potential, but not unbounded. What we either intuit or intuitively deny of the existence and meanings of "God" – that stubborn monosyllable – what we cannot translate or paraphrase out of pure mathematics, defines the immanence of language, its inevitable "infolding" (Darwin used the verb) inside the limits of our world. So does our incapacity to answer the questions: "What is music about?," "What does it signify?," "What in the world is it like?" Yet at the very same time, the walls which all discourse runs up against, theological-metaphysical, mathematical and musical, enforce on us undeniable intimations of the transcendent, of the unsayable presence, of the "other" across the border. Trapped within its measureless limitations, inside the fruitful immensity of its final failures – "Word, word that I lack," cries out Schoenberg's Moses in the face of the unspeakable – language posits negatively but overpoweringly the pressure, the "thereness" of what lies beyond it. As mystics insist, as daily experience so often confirms, the falling short of language makes absence substantive. What carries a moré vehement weight and feel of actual being than the capacity of syntax to attest that "there is a there there"?

Blocked at its far frontiers, yet pressed forward "from behind" by intuition, imagination, analysis, and evident sensation, which clamor for articulation, language, in regard to music, "messes about." It uses what glue, string, or rusty nails lie more or less to hand. Musical analysis, musicology, the history of music, and the narration of performance, breed their own technical idiom. In some spectral sense, a score is a translation, for the person trained to decipher it, of the musical-acoustic fact into a "meta-language" or executive code. But almost everything said about musical compositions by critics, by poets or writers of fiction, by the ordinary listener and music-lover is verbiage (in the pragmatic, even neutral sense of the word). It is talk which enlists metaphor, simile, analogy in a more or less impressionistic, wholly subjective magma.

Exceptionally acute and technically equipped commentators – a Tovey, an Adorno, a Hans Keller – can modulate their acoustic response, their analyses of the compositional process into a mimetic, "parallel" semantics. A Charles Rosen can edge verbal means closer to the untranslatability of the musical experience. Certain masters of exact hearing and of linguistic phrasing – of those tonal, rhythmic, harmonic lineaments in spoken and written speech which imply some kinship to music – are able to evoke, with tantalizing proximity, the actual effects of music on consciousness. Proust, for example, on "Vinteuil's sonata"; Joyce throughout *Ulysses;* Thomas Mann in his *Faustus.*

But only a handful of thinkers and "feelers" in language, in the evolution of reasoned argument, have had anything firsthand or defining to tell us about "what is music." They form a fascinating constellation: Augustine, Rousseau, Kierkegaard, Schopenhauer, Nietzsche, Adorno. A select paucity. It strikes one as almost scandalously rare in regard to a phenomenon of so manifest and universal a reality as is music; to a phenomenon without the which, for innumerable men and women, this plagued earth and our transit on it would probably be unbearable. As I see ("hear") it, one of the ways in which we can pay our debt to music, to its role in our lives, is to keep asking. How is it, Berkeley inquired, that we are driven to, that we somehow can conceive of the inconceivable, of that which denies the words, the grammars of discursive understanding? Music bears insistent witness to the question. In the face of music, the wonders of language are also its frustrations.

The challenge is not only that of the radical untranslatability of music. Even at their most intimate, the relations between music and language bristle with intractabilities. In Vico, in Rousseau, philosophic anthropology has it that music preceded speech. Birds, possibly certain marine mammals, sing, though we can only suspect that their songs communicate specific meanings. Winds, dunes, and rocks can sing. I have heard them do so in the Negev at the first cool of night. Schopenhauer affirms that if our universe was to cease, music would endure – a proposal incomprehensible on any rational, evidential level. Thus music would stand at the alpha and omega of *Sein,* of being itself. Its forms in motion are at once more immediate and freer than those of language. By uses of inversion, of counterpoint, of polyphonic simultaneity, music can house contradictions, reversals of temporality, the dynamic coexistence within the same overall movement of wholly diverse, even mutually denying moods and pulses of feeling. There inheres in language, at its generative foundations, an abdication from the manifold and the self-contrarieties of the world. Be it surrealistic, be it nonsense-verse, be it elevated to the pitch of visionary ecstasy, verbal discourse remains linear, sequential in time. It is hand-cuffed to the avarice of logic, with its ordinance of causality, with its (probably crass) segmentation of time and perception into past, present, and future. Identity principles, the end-stopping of sentences (mathematical proofs can be of infinite length), axioms of continuity, render speech and writing, however polysemic our words, however subtle and animate with fantastication our phrasing of the imaginary, despotic. We speak in (rich) monotones. Our poetry is haunted by the music it has left behind. Orpheus shrinks to a poet when he looks back, with the impatience of reason, on a music stronger than death.

Since that fatality, the word has sought to rival and to domesticate song. It has imitated musical means from inside itself. It knows rhythm, cadence, sonorities, echo-effects, changes of "key," thematic variations. It can, in some "measure" – itself a musical, choreographic rubric – modulate from one register of energy and mood to another. It has its treble and its bass, its whispers and its pedal-points. Rhetoric voices clarion-calls and drum-rolls. Mallarmé was a virtuoso of verbal wood-winds; Hopkins of percussion. But these are imperfect legacies and borrowings "by analogy." When words are set to music, when music is composed to a text, the primal conflict ensues. In every serious *Lied,* cantata, choral or operatic music-speech (*Sprechgesang* taken as a general category), the tension, the agonistic tug-of-war are palpable. The music aims, consciously or not, to draw back into its own totality, to drain of translatable lexical-grammatical sense, the text. It seeks to vocalize completely the phonetics, the signifying syllables of language. Words are to be melted into pure *vocalises*. In its competing turn, the lyric, the verbal *libretto,* the biblical passage, intends to achieve parity or, indeed, preeminence. The music is to be accompaniment. It is there to ornament, to project, to underline and "body forth" emotions, reflexes of sensibility, semantic contents ultimately linguistic. Yet music and dance are of themselves primordial motions and figurations of the human spirit which declare an order of being nearer than is language to the unknown of creation. We hear, we perceive in them what today's cosmology calls "the background noises," "the background radiation" of the primal burst out of nothingness. At the roots of grammar lie the fragmentations and, in a vital sense, diminutions of cerebral rationality, the fall of man into logic.

The two forces, that of music and that of language, quintessentially conflictual, meet in the human voice when it sings. Language can only yield abstractions or images when it attempts to define the cardinal wonder of a singing mouth (that mouth whose unquenchable song outlives Orpheus' death and decapitation). Song is simultaneously the most carnal and spiritual of realities. It enlists diaphragm and soul. It can, with its very first notes, reduce the listener to desolation or transport him to ecstasy. The singing voice can break or heal the psyche in a cadence. Organically, human song sets us closer to animality than any other manifestation. Messiaen dwells on this nearness. The literal bestiality of twentieth-century politics, the regression to inhumanity grunts and screams out of the pop-idol and rock-star. They are, whether we would or not, truth-screamers. At the other end of the gamut, a voice breathing into immediacy, say Schubert's *Winterreise* or the song out of the night in Mahler's Third, touches more intimately, steals closer to the border-crossing into "otherness," into the *terra incognita* of a humanity beyond itself than, perhaps, any experience else (unless it be that of the mystic, always uncertain). Song leads us home to where we have not yet been.

Nonetheless, even in the sources of song, as well as in those of instrumental music, the rivalries with language, a "strangeness" or *daimonia* in music when it collides with human speech-acts and consciousness, will out. Plato's fear of music had its rationale.

Strangeness comports violence. The three Greek myths – scholars regard them as among the most archaic – which narrate the origins of music, the primordial collisions between song and word, are replete with terror and blood. What shadows, older than history, can we make out in the sadistic flaying of Marsyas? Why do his pipes excite the panic of Athena and the unforgiving rage of Apollo, god of the lyre?

In certain Anatolian communities, to this day, string-players and performers on pipes and percussion live in apartheid or ritual enmity. The blown reed, immediate neighbor to the wind, the pipes of Pan, seem to mark the precarious transgression from nature to culture. In their range, we can hear the whistling of birds, the yelp of the fox. They can belong to the solitary, the illiterate, and those who cohabit, in an almost animal state, with their flocks. The shrill of the pipe, mimed by our piccolo, the tremolo of the flute, can suggest or echo a whiteness as of madness. In fatal contrast, Apollo's lyre is the instrument of reasoned harmony, of Pythagorean-mathematical relations and intervals. It is crafted out of slain animals – the shell of the tortoise, the gut of the cat. The lyre induces music towards speech, towards the textuality of the lyric, of epic recitation. The pipes of Marsyas are the "woodnotes wild" of ways of life a shade less than and prior to man; the Apollonian lyre is that of a thoroughly humanized, divinely inspired species. Between them ensues a homicidal rivalry.

Interpretations of the Sirens are never-ending. They have inspired iconography, music, literature, philosophic debate from archaic vase-paintings to Debussy, Kafka, Lampedusa, and the dialectics of the Frankfurt School. Birds or women or both? Fish-tailed (fish-headed in Margritte!) but armed with murdering claws. Did Odysseus really outwit their song at the cost of some irreparable dryness and mercantile utilitarianism henceforth in possession of his soul? Or did the Sirens fall silent at his passage (this being the silence which, according to Kafka, probably drawing on a hint in Rilke, no one can survive)? Ancient mythographers tell of a charnelhouse of human bones around their marine lair. One intuits in this grim, enigmatic fable an early chapter in the *agon,* in the struggle between music and word, between song and ratiocination. The Sirens strive to draw back into the tidal drag and deeps of music the usurpations, the claims to dominance of the *logos,* of syntax. The "language-animal," as the ancient Greeks designated man, new and cunning in his verbal devices, would reduce music to accompaniment, to "lyrics" or the minstrel's setting of heroic narrative. Odysseus is, precisely, the first virtuoso of rhetoric, of advocacy and circumlocution. He has escaped the Cyclops by means of a profound linguistic-logical ruse. With the suicide of the Sirens after their defeat at his cold hands, the *Ur*-alchemy of music, its truths outside and past reason, ebb from an aging world. Soon the mariners passing Samos will hear the cry: "The Great God Pan is dead." In Maurice Blanchot's memorable phrase, "ode" will have become "episode." But every time music insists on its absoluteness, rejecting any text, any program, any scenic or attendant function, it pays to the despair of the Sirens the homage of echo.

A considerable measure of literature and of literature set to music in the West stems directly from the matter of Orpheus. The connotations, the lineaments of possible significance in this myth are seemingly boundless. The shorthand, the fundamental encoding and mapping inward of our psyche seem to pivot on the constants of the confrontation between eros and death. They invoke a descent into darkness and return to the light – the rich nuances of resurrection – such as these are dramatized, with the economy of the measureless, in the Orpheus myth. Again, music and language, their intimacies and root-antagonism, are of the essence. Orpheus' art of poetry within song, the magic of his voice, compel nature and its wild creatures to gentle accord. Did Orpheus graft verse to music when he sang death into restitution? What, then, was his text? "Orphic" poets such as Rilke ask whether Eurydice desired rebirth, whether she had not found a warmer welcome and peace in the underworld. To this conjecture, Kafka appends a grim gloss: the most piercing music, the finest of songs is that of the condemned souls singing in the pit of hell.

Each of these three fathomless fables tells of laceration: Marsyas' bloody skin howls in the breeze; the bones of torn mariners bleach on the Siren-rocks; Orpheus is rent limb from limb by the Thracian women. Arthur Golding's renaissance version of Ovid drips with justified gore:

> . . . and then with bluddy hands
> They ran upon the prophet who among them singing stands.
> They flockt about him like as when a sort of birds have found
> An Owl a day tymes in a tod: and hem in full round,
> As when a Stag by hungrye hownds is in a morning found
> The which forestall him round about and pull him to the
>   ground.

Orpheus' members lie "in sundrie steds." But his head and harp will be washed up on Lesbos' strand, "the great mouth singing still."

Why this savagery, almost cannibalistic, in stories about the dawn of music and the birth of musical modes and instruments? I have said that vestiges of the original polemic between word and music are unmistakable. As are the ambiguities which attach to the wonder of the singing voice, part animal, part god. But I wonder whether the impulses of immemorial violence in these founding-myths are not indicative of a central, if opaque, insight. It is not only that there is in music a strangeness to man. In a value-free use of the term, music is informed by an elemental inhumanity (a "non-humanity").

It is alien to truth and falsehood. I know of no deeper, more neglected conundrum in epistemology, in semiotics and the cognitive *sciences de l'homme*. It is no accident that it is Nietzsche, inebriate with music, who posits "beyond good and evil," beyond the naïvety of "truth." Human speech can never do without falsehood. It may have arisen out of the necessities of fiction, of the manifold need "to say what is not" (Swift's lapidary phrase). Our subjunctives, our conditionals, our optatives, the "if" clauses in our grammars make possible an indispensable, radically human counter-factuality. They make it possible for us to alter, re-shape, fantasticate, cancel out the material constraints of our biological-empirical world. They are the woken dreams which give license to consciousness, which empower us to put into words the weather on the Monday morning after our own funeral. Thus all futurities, but also the articulation of remembrance, turn on the fictive genius of grammar. The "life-lie" (Ibsen) is language's irrecusable function, be it in the conventions of everyday social communication or at the heights of poetry and metaphysics.

Can music lie? To be sure, it can accompany, in operatic roles for example, a verbal falsity, suggesting, underlining its mendacious intent, comical or tragic. Consider the whole instrumentation of lies in Mozart's *Così fan tutte* or Verdi's *Falstaff.* But this is trivial. Can music, in its autonomy, be false? (False to what?) Can it be counter-factual and convey, by its own integral means, "that which is not the case"? Concomitantly, what are the "truth-functions" in music, in what sense can a musical statement be said to be "true"? (True to what?) The concordance between music and mathematics has been noted and put into practice since the pre-Socratics. It obtains on both a formal and performative level (measure, beat, division). But it breaks down at a decisive point. In mathematics, however pure, however speculative and detached from application, axioms, theorems, lemmas have to be shown to be true or false. This is the heart of proof. Spinoza read in mathematics the actual visage of truth. In music there can be violations of the declared contract with a chosen, rule-bound form such as a fugue or a canon. These can be labeled "errors" in a technical-conventional matrix. The beginner gets his exercises in counterpoint "wrong." But such errors or irregularities are in no sense a "falsehood" or a "lie." On the contrary: in the history of music, it is very often such breaches of contract with received technical conventions and auditive habits which generate innovation and development. The discords, the dissonances tested by Beethoven, the subversions of tonality in Liszt's late studies for the piano, beget modern atonal systems. They do not, they cannot "lie." When we say that they enrich and renew musical "truths," we are using this concept in a borrowed, undefinable manner.

Beyond true and false, beyond good and evil. The two dichotomies are closely, though complexly, intermeshed. Music can be abused when it is composed and executed in glorification of political tyranny, of commercial *kitsch*. It can be, indeed it has been, played loud enough to cover the cries of the tortured. Such abuse, of which exploitations of Wagner's music, but even of Beethoven's Ninth (we recall Adorno's jotting) are emblematic, is wholly contingent. It does not arise from, it does not negate the ontological and formal extraterritoriality of music to good and evil. In fear of Wagner, Lukács asked whether even a single bar of Mozart can be politically abused, can be made expressive of inherent evil. To which, when I reported the challenge, Roger Sessions, that most thoughtful of composers, replied by sitting down at his piano and playing the menace-aria of the Queen of the Night in *The Magic Flute*. Adding at once, however, "No, Lukács is right."

Thus men and women find themselves creating and experiencing a phenomenality, an almost limitless "fact" – the fact of music in its existential universality, for there is no culture or community without it – that is foreign to those axes of morality and of truth and non-truth which virtually organize all language and conscious reason. To "live music," therefore, as mankind has done since its inception, is to inhabit a realm which is, in its very essence, foreign to us. Hence, I venture, the afterglow, in our mythology, of auroral violence and the acknowledgment of a *mystère suprême.*

Yet it is precisely this realm which exercises over us "a sovereignty far greater than that of any other art" (Valéry). It is music which can invade and rule the human psyche with a penetrative strength comparable, it may be, only to that of narcotics or of the trance reported by shamans, saints, and ecstatics. Music can madden and it can help heal the broken mind. If it can be "the food of love," it can also trigger the feasts of hatred. A tune, a momentary cadence can come to possess our consciousness, it can cling to our recall whether we would or not, whether or not we were even aware of its spell when, often accidentally, we first heard it. Suddenly, as it were, it "hums our mind" and will not let go. Massed voices – the Welsh at rugby – bring on an unrivaled unison of communal fraternity; they generate shared prayer and meditation, paradoxically hushed in their very volume. But when harnessed to a national or partisan anthem, to the hammer-thrust of a march, the same choral practices, in an identical key, can unleash blind discipline, tribal mania, and collective fury. A solo voice, out of sight, arching from the dark or from the quiet of morning, can transmute the space, the density, the perceived tenor of the world. It is not only "cheap music," the cunning jingle of the crooner, the trash-tune on the electric guitar, that breaks the heart: it is a Monteverdi lament, the oboes in a Bach cantata, a Chopin ballade.

Composers have given various accounts of the process of composition, of the genesis of melodic and harmonic discovery. We can ponder Beethoven's sketch-books and, at times, follow step by step the intricate, self-correcting advance towards what will, when realized, seem obvious. Or we can attend to Wagner's recollection of the incipience, in half-sleep, on a drowsy afternoon at La Spezzia, of the E-minor chord from which the architecture of the *Ring* unfolds. Nevertheless, even such first-hand testimony, either formal or metaphoric, provides little substantive insight into the musical act, into the provocation, itself so often unsolicited, sudden, and accidental, of vocal or instrumental constructs, energies, deployments out of "non-being." This is the puzzle: where does the new melody, the novel key-relation, the new "dynamic cell and cluster" (Boulez) originate? What, if you will, was there before? Silence, perhaps, but a silence which, in a linguistically inexpressible way, was not mute. Which was charged with "unresolved tensions and disequilibrium," as Roger Sessions put it, aching for release and resolution. A pent-up breath in the non-logical, counter-verbal synapses of the pre-conscious analogous to Aristotle's *entelechy*, that thirst towards form and fulfillment. Again, however, all these are similes, narratives of analogy which say more about the limits of language than they do about music.

What of the impact on us of music? What explanation have we for an experience at once utterly familiar, banal, quotidian, and "beyond words" – which is to say beyond adequate logical-rational explication? Tempi, volume, the tone-color of different voices and instruments (we are already in the metaphoric) obviously engender some kind of psychosomatic resonance in us. As do associations with sensorial and natural phenomena, the pulse of wind and water in Debussy, the texture of thickening night in a nocturne. Musical keys and modulations do appear to arouse certain respondent moods or emotions. But is this, primarily, a matter of historical convention, of schooled expectation? What makes a minor third "sad"? Is G-minor, in the Western scale, intrinsically *triste* (and just what could such a statement signify?), or does its desolation stem from the use Mozart makes of it in his great Quintet (K. 516)? What of the reflexes of sensibility motivated by keys, pitch, chordal blocks in non-Western tonic systems? Is a pentatonic structure any less universal than ours?

Attempts at a psychology, at a neurology and physiology of the workings of music on mind and body go back to Pythagoras and therapeutic magic. Plato worries acutely over the effects on the soul and society of diverse modes. The intuition that consciousness, together with subconsciousness and the human body are implicated, that music bonds with the "internet"of our receptors in some immensely subtle yet imperious chemistry, lies to hand. Endeavors to refine this intuition, to analyze its causal sequence, to verify it experimentally remain, until now, rudimentary. As do answers to the obvious question of differences of human response to the same music, of trenchant disagreements in emotional reflexes and value-judgments. Neither on logical nor substantive grounds can one *refute* the assertion that Mozart was an indifferent music-maker or that Monteverdi's *Vespers of the Virgin* are inferior to the croonings of Madonna. The more captive our delight, the more insistent our need of and "answering to" a piece of music, the more inaccessible are the reasons why. It is a platitude to observe that music shares with love and with death the mystery of the self-evident. This triad is a cliché, of which composers and writers on music have availed themselves prodigally. But it may be a cliché of essential suggestion.

As I have said in respect of the three myths, I believe that the overpowering, ubiquitous force and necessity of music has its source near the paradox of its intimate strangeness to man. It has its prologue in the organic and animal worlds. It is uniquely expressive of the highest states of human consciousness. It functions outside truth and falsehood, good and evil. It possesses men and women but is not possessed by them. Its "ligaments" with empirical, intelligible reality largely elude us. Even the purest mathematics can, in theory or by historical, contingent development, become applied. Music is only "applied" when it is adulterated. Certain theologies or metaphysical paradigms seek to conceptualize God as thought thinking itself, as absolute will willing itself into being and creation. Leibniz took music to be God's algebra. I have mentioned that late twentieth-century astrophysics seeks out wisps of matter left over from the "Big Bang," noises still audible in the background of time. In blameless analogy, one might define music as the soliloquy of being, of the original *fiat* echoing itself. But again, such intimations are, in the rigorous and etymological sense of the word, verbiage.

All I know is that music is a *sine qua non* in my existence. It reinsures what I sense to be or, rather, search for in the transcendental. This is to say that it demonstrates to me the reality of a presence, of a factual "thereness," which defies either analytic or empirical circumscription. This reality is at once commonplace, everyday, palpable, and ulterior. It exercises over us a singular domination. Neither psychoanalysis nor deconstruction nor post-modernism have had anything revelatory to say of music. This is crucial. These language-games of subversive decipherment, of suspicion in the wake of Nietzsche and of Freud, are virtually impotent before music. They remain arrogantly trapped within the language-sphere which they claim to relativize or unravel. Why should we take them seriously on the philosophic, on the human level?

A larger inference can be drawn. As it was by Wittgenstein when he recorded that, more than once, the slow movement in Brahms's Third Quartet pulled him back from the brink of suicide. Music authorizes, invites the conclusion that the theoretical and practical sciences, that rational investigation will never map experience exhaustively. That there are phenomena "at the center" (consciousness itself may be another) which will endure, boundlessly alive and indispensable, but "outside." This is, quite straightforwardly, the proof of the *meta*-physical. Music is significant to the utmost degree; it is also, strictly considered, meaningless. There abides its "transgression" beyond intellect.

My inability to sing or play an instrument humbles me. But music often puts me "beside myself" or, more exactly, in company far better than my own. It empowers the oxymoron of love, that fusion into a measure of oneness of two human persons each of whom, even at the moment of spiritual and sexual unison, remains, is made more richly himself or herself. To listen to music with the loved one is to be in a condition simultaneously private, almost autistic, yet strangely welded to another (shared reading, reading aloud, does not achieve this). Thus the collaborative inter-play as between voice and piano in a *Lied*, or the execution of a string quartet, may well be the most intricate, non-analyzable happening on this planet. It may be more complex, each incidence being non-repeatable, than is the dance of the galaxies. A var-nished sound-box, cat-gut or wire, a felt-tipped hammer, the in-flection of the player's wrist, the vibration of vocal cords generate waves whose algebraic curves and function we can, indeed, plot, but whose "signifiers," whose power to transmute physical and psychic states, we cannot account for. At their source, these powers are, I conjecture, "in"-human.

It is this which renders constantly fascinating the interactions between music and the other arts, between music and poetry. In pre-classical Greece, the philosopher could also be a rhapsode. He sang his thoughts. To our day, philosophic argument – in Plato, in Nietzsche, sometimes in Wittgenstein – can have its distinct musi-cality and cadence. That architecture is "frozen music," that po-etry aspires to the condition of music which is that of a perfect tautology of form and content – in music form is content and content is form – are shorthand assertions of deeply felt but un-reasoned truths. Who can define "the soul"? But who does not grasp intuitively Shakespeare's warning about those who "have no music in their souls," a warning crystallized in the designation "soul-music"?

I evade trying even to imagine the constraints, the human wretchedness inflicted by blindness, but ask myself whether deaf-ness would (will?) not be the darker darkness.

7

My mother, so Viennese, habitually began a sentence in one language and ended it in another. She seemed unaware of the dazzling modulations and shifts of intent which this produced. Languages flew about the house. English, French, and German in the dining and drawing-rooms. My nannie's "Potsdam" German in the nursery; Hungarian in the kitchen where, by accident or design, a succession of Magyar ladies – I remember them as voluminous and choleric – prepared my father's favorite dishes. I have no recollection of any first or bed-rock language. Later attempts to excavate one from within me, psychological tests, the hypothesis that the tongue in which I cried out to my wife when we were in a car mishap must be the linguistic base, have proved vain (even in moments of panic or shock, the language used is contextual, it is that of the speech-partner or locale). Whether it be in daily usage or mental arithmetic, in reading-comprehension or dictation, French, German, and English have been to me equally "native." Almost invariably, I simply dream in the language in which I happen to have spoken, which I happen to have mainly heard during the day. It is as if even the semantic subconscious is linguistically circumstantial in a somewhat obvious and material way.

Quite naturally, there are momentary lapses from fluency, of lexical or grammatical immediacy and resource when I have been, for any length of time, out of hearing, out of regular address of one or another of my three "mother-tongues." Moreover, there can be involuntary interference-effects, the one language interposing, insisting on primacy in the midst of the other. The sense is that of a brusque tear in a lattice of shot silk. The idiom needed, the turn of syntax seems, suddenly, to spring from the other tongue. Ordinarily, however, the three are at parity and will, when required, keep their integral distance from each other. I have lived trilingually. Whatever other language I manage to make myself understood in or to read has been added later, in the common process of acquisition.

Contrary to loose opinion, such a polyglot condition is by no means rare. Numerous cultures and societies are thoroughly bilingual – for example, in contiguous regions of Sweden and Finland, in Malaysia, in Hispanic communities in North America. Trilingualism is more unusual, but it exists. It can be found in Friulia, in those border-valleys of Switzerland and north-eastern Italy where local forms of *romanche,* main-line Italian, and Friulian (Pasolini's beloved medium) are current, presumably from earliest childhood. During lengthy periods of history, men and women had to be bilingual, communicating in their own local idiom – which can range all the way from patois and dialect to linguistic autonomy, as, for example, in the language spoken in Bergamo – and in the politically-economically dominant *lingua franca.* Until late into the eighteenth century, the educated throughout western Europe, but also in Warsaw or in Prague, be they scholars, philosophers, divines, scientists, men of law, diplomats, politicians, men of letters, shared Latin when in discourse with each other while being, simultaneously, practitioners of their own vulgate. It would be fascinating to know whether it was in Latin or in English that Newton analyzed inwardly and initially verbalized (conceptualized) his axioms. Spinoza and Leibniz almost certainly did so in Latin. Many of the perplexities which arise out of the epistemology of Descartes stem from the fact that Latin was the first language of his meditations, that translation into his native French proved recalcitrant also to himself. There is, on the other hand, scarcely a passage in the pedal-point English of *Paradise Lost* or in Milton's prose which does not bear witness to the Latin substratum and to the enriching intervention of other tongues (Italian among them).

These are visible summits. Largely lost to us, but undoubtedly ubiquitous, was the role of every type and nuance of multilingualism in the daily business, communal texture, evolutions of sensibility of ordinary human experience across the globe. It may well be that an authentically monoglot consciousness is historically and culturally the exception. Linguistic chauvinism, the exaltation of the official national tongue and its mythical roots, comes late. In the European instance, they hardly predate the sixteenth century. Today's planetary prepotence of Anglo-American, to which I will revert, is a crisis-phenomenon altering the very nature of language and human relations. Ironically, it too is generating an enforced bilingualism (the native speaker has to know both his tongue and Anglo-American).

The issue is of utmost significance. So-called progressive doctrines of child-rearing and of child-psychology, most notably in the United States, have opposed any early multilingualism. The more or less conscious chauvinism and pressure for ethnic integration operative in this pedagogy are obvious. The child is to be made a monoglot citizen, purged of his immigrant past, cleansed of the socially-professionally inhibiting legacy left to him by alien and lesser cultures. A standardized American English, pervasive from birth, will ensure access to the escalator of patriotism and success, to that hegemony of values and desires which the formidably imitable American way of life has come to exercise over so much of the earth. But the educational psychologist aims deeper.

In its consequent version, the argument has it that multilingualism from an early age will generate confusion in the nascent psyche; that it can induce personality disorders extending from benign muddle to something like outright schizophrenia. Segmented and confused between different tongues, the mind, the ligaments of coherent identity in the child will be partially or generally unraveled. Self-recognition will be obscured by conflictual streams of consciousness. No less damagingly, the child, the mature individual, will find it more and more arduous to assimilate with his or her "peer-group" and national heritage. A stranger to himself or herself, the linguistically uncentered man or woman may remain an alien in the midst of his or her American-style, liberal, egalitarian, materially blessed polity.

I hold this view to verge on idiocy. When applied, it beggars and domesticates the human spirit. Nevertheless, it does testify to an immemorial trauma. To that incident at Babel.

Anthropologists and ethnographers teach us that there is almost no culture, no ethnic community known whose mythology does not include some form of the Babel-motif. Incised, as it were, in human mentality, in the narratives which define historical and social identity, is the remembrance of a primal severance, of a brutal weaning. At creation, mankind was blessed with a single tongue. This Adamic esperanto was tautological in respect of truth and the world. This is to say that the objects, the conditions of perception and predication met with in reality corresponded exactly, point-to-point, as in a soluble equation, with the terms used to name and describe them. Adam nominates, gives a name to, all living creatures. These names, in turn, are an exact and total delineation of their essence. There can be no misprision, let alone falsehood. On his own scale, proportionate to that of God, man "speaks being"; he gives meaning to form as did the creator's *fiat*.

This semantics of informing verity, of absolute fit between word and world, enables mortals to understand, to answer to the speech of God or the gods. In numerous mythologies, this communicative immediacy extends to the animal-order. Although it is itself rudimentary and essentially mimetic, the language of birds and beasts is intelligible to man. A network of unifying articulation, of shared meaning, unfolds from creation – itself, not only in Judaic cosmology, a speech-act. The limits of the world are indeed, though in a sense other than Wittgenstein's, the limits of language. The mapping is both total and truthful.

Disaster strikes. The fatality can be of the most diverse sorts. In a congeries of Amerinidian tales, a sacred, totemic animal is accidentally or intentionally slain. In other, widely dispersed cultures, the cause is incest or the violation of some other primal taboo. The scenario of guilt points to man's illicit pursuit of knowledge, of some ultimate secret reserved solely for the gods or tutelary spirits (this is a characteristically Hebraic-Hellenic theme). The Torah legend of Babel, one of the most fragmentary and riddling in the canon, intimates *hubris,* some Promethean arrogance aimed at the hidden fabric of the heavens. Does the high tower recall the astronomical observatories of the Babylonian *ziggurat?*

Whatever the precise sin, retribution is pulverizing. The great serpent which had enfolded and harmonized creation is cut into innumerable pieces. The tower is hammered into dust. These are the images of a greater fracture. *Homo sapiens sapiens* no longer speaks a single, "truth-functional" language. An accursed babble infects his works and days. He is no longer in ontological concurrence with the facts of the world. Word and object, thought and articulation, feeling and communication no longer mesh organically. There are henceforth constant, intractable slippages between signifier and signified, between intention and executive form. We can never say the whole of what we mean, we can never purify verbal description or analysis of a possible penumbra of ambiguity, of inchoate or private values and connotations finally inexpressible. The adjective "unspeakable" vibrates obscurely with that intimation of an unresolved, muted urgency. Even at its most scrupulous or inspired, discourse approximates. We are no longer fully at home in our saying.

Concomitantly, the dialogue with the divine becomes the unanswered monologue of supplication. It no longer echoes or is receptor of the Word. Every major theological-metaphysical tradition tells of a time when direct colloquy with God and the springs of being ceases. Prophecy shrivels to prognostication. Seers are made soothsayers. Only the rarest of saints or heroes, a Saint Francis, a Siegfried, can now converse with the creatures of the field or the forest. Language has retracted into the parishes of what is merely human, local, and functional.

These parishes, moreover, are *incommunicado*. As the "Babel"-myths make graphic, nations, tribes, communities now confront each other in mutual incomprehension. They listen to each other's mouthings as if the infirm or deranged were moving their lips. The consequences have been incalculable. Reciprocal incomprehension breeds contempt. The Greek word *barbarian* taunts those whose tongue is rebarbatively incomprehensible. Ethnic hatred can follow on contempt. On a higher plane, attempts to search out the truth, to formulate and teach it – the philosophic enterprise – run into the fog of language(s). Spinoza affirms that error, controversy, mutual misinterpretation, arise ineluctably from the incapacity of different languages to grasp, to translate rightly, each other's vocabulary and grammar. Where divine creation had woven a seamless garment of truth-telling, the catastrophe at Babel has left a patchwork-quilt of approximations, misprisions, lies, and parochialism. Eminent spirits have urged mankind to undo Babel. Is there, for shared use, any tongue in which vestiges of the Adamic, of universal truth to being, subsist? Hebrew, Greek, Chinese have had their proponents. Can a new unifying, all-embracing idiom be edified – a Leibnizian symbol-calculus, an esperanto, a computer code? Surely, the manifest answer to our economically-socially dispersed, wasteful, even dangerous linguistic circumstance is the adoption of a planetary tongue – that is, basic American English. The benefits of such standardization are dazzling: not only on the economic-scientific-technological front, where it is already largely in force, but on the vital level of a better understanding between races, nations, ideologies. Chinese and Russian plenipotentiaries negotiate in American English; so do Arab and Israeli. The ancient curse can (must) be exorcised.

I do not recall when first I misread Genesis II. Mythographers, long before Freud, knew that fables can conceal their original, primal sense; that they can, indeed, reverse it altogether. Enthralled by the play and marvel of languages, I felt, already as a child, that the story of Babel was a "coverup"; that it inverted a more ancient and true meaning. Straining to celebrate God's cosmic monarchy, the tribes had gathered to build a sublime sky-scraper, a spiraling ascent which could bring their worship closer to his celestial omnipotence. To reward this worshipful labor, the Lord had, albeit in His somewhat brusque and veiled fashion, bestowed on man the incommensurable gift of tongues. He had given to men and women the light, the inexhaustible wealth of Pentecost. Far from being a malediction, the cornucopia of different languages poured out on the human species constituted a blessing without end. Surely, a moment's thought made this obvious.

Our biological-somatic condition is quintessentially bounded. It is end-stopped by personal extinction. It is a perpetual hostage to infirmity, illness, decay, and limitation. The newborn is old enough to die (Montaigne). A shop-worn but justifiable rhetoric insists on the brevity, brutishness, ugliness, or fundamental boredom of the vast majority of lives, on the "quiet desperation," as Thoreau put it, and not always quiet, which inhabits all but exceptional hours, illusions, or epiphanies in any common *vita*. An irrefutable realism empowers the archaic Greek postulate whereby "It is best not to be born and next best to die young," old age being, with so very few exceptions, a malodorous waste, an incontinence of mind and body made raw by the remembrance of the unfulfilled.

What, then, is the well-spring of our ineradicable hopes, of our intimations of futurity, of our forward-dreams and utopias, public and private? Whence the radiant scandal of our investments in tomorrow, in after-tomorrow? Which is the source of "the life-lie," the gamble on improbability which makes most individuals and societies, despite recurrent exceptions, reject the logic of despair and of suicide? In short: from where rises the high tide of desire, of expectation, of an obsession with sheer being defiant of the pain, of the treadmill of enslavement and injustice, of the massacres that are history?

It is my conviction that these liberations from the constraints of the physical, from the blank wall of our own death and a seeming eternity of personal and collective disappointment, are in crucial measure linguistic. Bio-socially, we are indeed a short-lived mammal made for extinction, as are all other kinds. But we are a *language*-animal, and it is this one endowment which, more than any other, makes bearable and fruitful our ephemeral state. The evolution in human speech – it may have come late – of subjunctives, optatives, counter-factual conditionals and of the futurities of the verb (not all languages have tenses) has defined and safeguarded our humanity. It is because we can tell stories, fictive or mathematical-cosmological, about a universe a billion years hence; it is because we can, as I mentioned, discuss, conceptualize the Monday morning after our cremation; it is because "if"-sentences ("If I won the lottery," "If Schubert had lived to a ripe age," "If a vaccine is developed against AIDS") can, spoken at will, deny, reconstruct, alter past, present, and future, mapping *otherwise* the determinants of pragmatic reality, that existence continues to be worth experiencing. Hope is grammar. The mystery of futurity or freedom – these two are intimately kindred – is syntactical. Optatives, the grammatical modes of desideration, open the prison house of physiological necessity, of mechanical laws. Is there any more concise nomination of utopia than that of the French verb form, *le plus-que-parfait*? Ought one not to pause in constant amazement at the capacity of preterites to reconstruct history as well as one's personal past? This wondrous turn is compacted in the famous untranslatability of the opening sentence of Proust's *A la Recherche*. Yet even these grammatologies of emancipation yield to the miracle, for surely it is nothing less, of the future of "to be," of the "shall" and the "will" whose articulation generates the breathing-spaces of fear and of hope, of renewal and innovation which are the cartography of the unknown.

Consider a language, a consciousness confined to the present tense, to factuality of the most tautological, "truth-functional" register. With caustic ambivalence, Swift both exalts such a tongue of blank veracity, and assigns it to horses. What tedium of persistent noon must have attended on the shadowless truth of Adamic speech. How flat is an immortality of the present. It is the instrumentalities of the imaginary, of the unverifiable (the poetic), it is the potentiality of fictions (lies) and syntax-leap into tomorrows without end, which have made of men and women, of women and men babblers, gossips, poets, metaphysicians, planners, prophets, and rebels against death.

Thus it was not only pain, guilt, mortality, and a life-sentence at hard labor which came with ostracism from Eden. It was the central dynamics of hope (what is there to hope for in the Garden, in the Disney-world of the divine?). Together with music, language, any language, has in it these infinite resources of being. It is the supreme gift to and gift of man. It makes possible the building of towers half-way to the stars.

No language is, formally, measurable. In analogy with the organic, it undergoes incessant change. Languages live and die. They manifest epochs of enrichment, of acquisition, of political-cultural-literary dominance, and epochs of diminution and decay. They tend to divide into dialects which may become autonomous and originate a new language. They can also be absorbed into larger, more forceful clusters. No lexicon, no grammar fixes or describes exhaustively a natural language. Semantic components interact, often randomly, like molecules at the surface of a liquid.

Each and every human tongue is different. This is the overwhelming fact. Each and every natural language constitutes an integral world. It may be, as transformational-generative theories of grammar maintain, that certain deep structures of a wholly formal, meta-mathematical tenor generate rules and constraints valid for all languages. Moreover, it seems evident that *homo sapiens* had to develop and share certain physiological attributes so as to produce, to voice articulate speech (we will require oxygen in order to breathe). Such innate deep structures – the theory remains unproved – and physiological equipment are, undoubtedly "universals." They are, at once, axiomatic and, in regard to the actual linguistic situation, trivial. The formal algorithms of a universal grammar relate to the measureless prodigality and differentiation of human tongues after Babel, as does taxidermy to a lion in progress.

No two languages, no two dialects or local idioms within a language, identify, designate, map their worlds in the same way. The memories stored, the empirical surroundings inventoried, the social relations which the language organizes and mirrors (kinship, for example), the colors distinguished in its vocabulary of perceptions, differ, often radically, from tongue to tongue. Immediately neighboring tongues, even in the same climatic-geophysical locale, will differ to the pitch of total mutual incomprehension. These are "isolates" within galaxies of structurally cognate languages (e.g., Basque, certain languages in the Philippines). To speak a language is to inhabit, to construct, to record a specific world-setting – a *mundanity* in the strong, etymological sense of the word. It is to occupy and traverse a singular landscape in time. A dictionary is the most alive and comprehensive of atlases. The stratigraphy, the many-layered provenance of a word, of an idiomatic phrase, encapsulates the *Lebensraum*, the memories privileged or suppressed, the laws and literature of a community and culture. Consider the *Littré* or the *Oxford English Dictionary*. Languages will conserve, with uncanny tenacity, names of trees, of fauna from lands they have long abandoned. They preserve configurations of mores and institutions long past and almost indecipherable to the present.

In no two languages are these processes of inheritance and of innovation the same. The "simpler" the terms, the more intractable the task of absolute transfer. (Are there any "simple" terms or, as Roman Jakobson would ask his dumbstruck students, "What do you mean by a literal sense?") The stored remembrance of availability, even of plenty in *bread* (cf. the American black use of the word to signify "money"), is at many points contrary to the overtones of want, of mutinous hunger in *pain.* There is an untranslatable excess of history, of proprietary mystique in German *Heimat.* The precise inference of "heart," of a ceremonious bent of spirit in Italian *cortesia* tell of an anatomy of feeling, of muted ritual now eroded but once pivotal to Tuscan culture. So far as is known, it is exceedingly rare for any language to situate the past as being "in front of" the speaker. An Indian tongue in the high Andes is said to do just this. The logic is impeccable. We can see the past, we back into the unknown future as does Paul Klee's storm-driven *Angelus Novus* of history (talismanic to Walter Benjamin). The belief that North African Arab speech contains a dozen terms for species of desert sand or that there are some twenty words for "snow" in Eskimo languages, is a popular delusion. What matters is that in both cases the available vocabulary will comprise a wealth of exact discrimination, of psychologically, materially, and socially recognized density and shading absent from other languages. Names of objects, even those most evidently commonplace, are "worlds apart." Inland, Odysseus' oar is mistaken for, which is to say translated into, a winnowing-fan.

Every tongue ever spoken by men and women, where "tongue" includes dialects, professional idioms, argot, the discourse of different social classes and generations within the same *communitas,* opens its own window on life and the world. The room behind the window has been designed and furnished by the relevant language. Which is reflected, sometimes to the point of opacity, by the window-panes. In turn, the world perceived, named, surveyed, reflects back into the room, into the given "speech-space." The resulting dialectic is one of incessant exchange. Of this interaction the history (diachronic) and current means (synchronic) of a language are made. Strangely, there are languages which do seem to stand regularly at open windows, whereas others appear to look inward or through narrow shutters. But in either instance, the acts of vision and revision are autonomous to the language. The light is never that of any other.

If one rejects notions of catastrophe or supernatural chastisement, what explanation can there be for this prodigality? From a rational, utilitarian, practical perspective, this plethora is crazy. The waste of communicative ease which attaches to it is drastic. The social, economic, political benefits of mutual comprehension, the rigor of definition and consensus – scientific, philosophic, but also domestic – to be derived from a single world-language, from a unified syntax, are self-evident. In the name of common sense, what possible justification can there be for the mushrooming on this small globe of an estimated 20,000 different tongues? Let me sharpen the conjecture set out in *After Babel* (1975).

To account for the fantastic multiplicity of natural species, often on minute territories (100,000 species of insects in a corner of Amazonia), Darwinian theory invokes the mechanism of adaptation. Every species represents a more or less exact "fit," filling a specific niche, as if nature did indeed abhor a vacuum. Of this seeming excess and differentiation comes the teeming energy of organic being and development. The linguistic analogue suggests itself. Each and every human tongue enacts one of a presumably open-ended spectrum of possibilities. These possibilities are the readings of time and of the world to which I have referred. German *Weltanschauung* is precisely right. A language fills a niche in the honeycomb of potential perceptions and interpretations. It articulates a construct of values, meanings, suppositions which no other language exactly matches or supersedes. Because our species has spoken, speaks in manifold, diverse tongues, it engenders the wealth of environments and adapts to them. We speak world*s*.

Thus Babel was the contrary of a curse. The gift of tongues is

precisely that; a gift and benediction beyond reckoning. The riches
of experience, the creativities of thought and of feeling, the penetrative and delicate singularities of conception made possible by
the polyglot condition are the preeminent adaptive agency and
advantage of the human spirit. Every lexicon, every grammar, be
they unwritten, embodies the means of evolutionary discovery in
thought, in law, in the narratives which shape time. A language
casts over the thronged seas of encountered totality its own particular net. With this net, it draws to itself riches, depths of insight, life-
forms which would, otherwise, remain unrealized. (There are affinities of privation, though grimly different in degree, between the
monoglot and the mute.) Whatever its drawbacks in respect of
facile communication, of the "internet" of practical profit, the
prodigality of tongues after Babel is a "Darwinian transcendent." It
is a cause for jubilation. I felt this, with an almost bodily intensity,
already as a child.

The varieties of religious beliefs and experience, the Aladdin's
cave of cosmogonies, what Wallace Stevens called the "supreme
fictions" of our philosophies and metaphysics, relate immediately
to linguistic diversities. They are built of language(s). Our literatures are children of Babel. The final untranslatability of a poetic
or philosophic text (I will return to this point) declares the *genius
loci* internalized by each and every tongue. The interplay, scarcely
explored, between eros and discourse, dramatizes the privilege of
the polyglot.

We intuit the depths at which the utterance of desires and
imaginings to and between sexual partners interact with physiology, with the quality, cadence, and aura of intercourse. But we
know next to nothing of the actual psychosomatic interface at
which speech and sex enter into conjoined performance. Are there
connections between speech-centers and synapses in the cortex

and the parasympathetic nerve-system? What we do know is this: the auto-suggestions (masturbatory), the tropes, the transgressed taboos and argotic carnival of sex-speech, both in soliloquy and dialogue, are seminal components of the sexual act itself. We speak sex, to ourselves and to others before, often during and after intercourse or orgasm. French *jactance,* pulsing emission, applies both to eloquence and to the erotic.

Sexual rhetoric differs radically from language to language. Every language, every historical period and social context within that language will, for example, draw the line of the verbally "forbidden," of the unsayable or linguistically subterranean, at different levels on the lexical scale. What is light bawdy in one tongue, is taboo and darkest-night idiom in another (compare the histories of *con/*"cunt" in French and in English). No two languages prepare identical cartographies of the human body and its elected privacies. The rhythms, the accelerandos or adagios of gesture which organize the intricate choreography of human persons in the process of sexual relations, are cadenced by words. The stimulus of voiced intimacies is linguistic-specific. It varies from speech-community to speech-community, from literacy to literacy. It extends from the pre-packaged cliché and crassness of the four-letter chant in the Anglo-Saxon populist matrix to such high inventions as Proust's *faire Catléya.* To make love in American English, say, is a complexly different happening for the articulate from doing so in German, in Italian, or in Russian (*Lolita* hints magically at these distinct kingdoms). The eros of the multilingual, even that of a monoglot endowed with verbal means and ear, differs from that of the linguistically underprivileged or the tone-deaf. At one extreme, we find the stuttering rage, the sexual suffocation so paradoxically expressive in Büchner's *Wozzeck*; at the other, a veritable Don Juanism of tongues – that inescapably

linguistic-erotic instrument – which celebrates Babel. How mono-
tone must love-making have been in Paradise.

Are there disadvantages to being a traveler between languages, a
double, triple, or even quadruple agent across frontiers of identity?
It is sometimes asserted that only the monoglot or the individual
uncompromisingly rooted in his one native language will have
access to its full range and deeps. The polyglot, however sensitive
to nuance and specificity, will never possess that somnambular at-
homeness in a single tongue which marks not only the writer (the
poet first and foremost) but also the receptive reader and critic of a
literary text. A final complicity in the basic structures and "quid-
dity" of the language will elude him.

This belief was murmured to me with unctuous venom by
elements in the English Faculty of Cambridge University during
the 1960s. It has been a raucous shibboleth in racist, nationalist,
and tribal ideologies and "cleansing" programs since the nineteenth century. Only the native speaker can proclaim, at mystical
depths, the *Blut und Boden,* the *terre et les morts* of the race or
nation-state. In its modern guise, this claim goes back to Herder
and the romantic nationalism unleashed by the French Revolution
and the Napoleonic saga. Communal and personal coherence, the
identity and historicity of the culture are inalienably bound to the
genius of the language as it surges from the tenebrous well-spring
of the ethnic source. No outsider, no courier or carrier of contra-
band between tongues, even where such portage occurs from earliest childhood and inside the same psyche, can wholly belong.

There *may* be a grain of truth in this dictate. It is at least
arguable that certain categories of poetry or of fiction derive their
immediacy, their seemingly subconscious enlistment of etymology
and connotations deep-buried, from total, interference-free im-

mersion in the native idiom. In Thomas Hardy's verse, for example, in Faulkner's novels, something of the strength and lapidary
weight of the language seems to declare the salutary absence of any
"contamination" from without. It is of its "earth earthy."

The actual history of Western literature (and of philosophy and
the sciences) does, however, point the other way. Linguistic chauvinism, the striving for official-pedagogic purification, so absurdly
pursued by French governments and academicians, are recent,
post-romantic reflexes. As I said, intellectual Europe is bilingual in
respect of Latin till the late eighteenth century. Milton is exquisitely at home in Italian; his 1645 book of poems, perhaps the
most accomplished in English literature, is multilingual. Clairvoyant as to the mounting threats of nationalism, Goethe states
flatly that no monoglot truly knows his own language.

Today, and fascinatingly, certain currents in literature are again
polyglot, precisely as they were throughout the European Middle
Ages and Renaissance. Joseph Conrad and Oscar Wilde, bilingual
in their creativity, marginal and peregrine in their existence, are
instrumental in this turn. To cite only the pre-eminent, Borges,
Nabokov, and Beckett move between tongues with utter virtuosity. In Beckett's *oeuvre,* we often cannot be certain as to the
language of the *Ur*-text, let alone as to that of its mental genesis.
There is not much recent Anglo-American critical prose or response to poetry more assured than Joseph Brodsky's. The notion
that these men are somehow disadvantaged, alienated in or by
their chosen tongues, is palpably silly.

On a level self-evidently minor, I owe to the cross-weave of
three initial languages, to their pulse and flicker within me, the
very conditions of my life and work. It is for others to judge
whether interference-effects between these threefold identities and

whatever I have added from other tongues (a long love-affair and comedy of errors in and with Italian) have disqualified my writings, and if so in what ways. Or whether, as I believe, it is the meaning of their meaning. The rewards have been emphatic. There is a perpetual joy, a touch of wonder, to writing in English, in French, in German; to teaching in these three; to being deemed, in the French case peremptorily, as resident in each. And can there be for any writer, for any "thinker" – that French and German rubric so grating on Anglo-American ears – a better hour than that spent with his or her translators, modulating from the language in which an essay or book was composed to another, also his or hers? Translation, that harvest out of Babel, is indeed of the essence.

It has busied my entire working life. Every act and motion of meaning (the semiotic realm) comports translation. The form can be oral or graphic or symbolic; it can be a semaphore signal or a metaphysical disquisition. The receiver "translates," has to translate what he hears, reads, or perceives. Preeminently, he does so within his own tongue. Translation is, first and foremost, intralingual. It serves to decipher messages between speakers and writers within the same speech-community. Usually, such reciprocal decipherment occurs without conscious notice, though the actual process is exceedingly complicated – and always astonishing. Often, however, it should invite deliberate attention. Children and adults translate each other's idiom, as do successive generations. Language is in perpetual motion and mutation. Regions, even neighboring villages have their own dialects and pronunciations (the Venetian lagoon is Babel). So do social classes. These differences generate diverse identities and codes of intent. The meeting of accent with accent, of inflection with inflection, necessitates interpretations (translations) of political-ideological values, of contrasting historical remembrance and allusion, of hopes (future tenses) which differ subtly or radically. Linguistic exchanges between men and women are, all too often, a contract for misunderstanding.

This constant stream of translation, moreover, is perhaps never meant to be a final decoding. Each and every human being speaks an "idiolect": this is to say a language, a "parlance" which remains in some of its lexical, grammatical, and semantic aspects his or her own. With time, with individual experience, these aspects incorporate associations, connotations, accretions of intimate memory, privacies of reference singular to the speaker or writer. For each one of us, there are tone-clusters, particular words, phrases either embedded in our consciousness or branching, as it were, into the subconscious, whose patterns of sense, whose specific charge is deeply ours. These elements translate only partially in even the most scrupulous proceedings of shared communication. All exchanges remain incomplete. Scarcely investigated is the intricate play of soliloquy. We harbor different voices inside us. These can enact different language-games. In the strident babble or silence of schizophrenia, the minimal conditions of inward commerce break down. But into what?

Interlingual translation, the enterprise after Babel, merely replicates, on a scale of heightened visibility and purpose, the model of transfer within any single tongue. Its requirements and impossibilities – at the total, ideal pitch – are exactly those we experience, with less awareness, less acutely, when trying to make and to trade sense in our everyday, native discourse. The schematic project – emission of the message, reception via ear and eye, interpretative decipherment, response – is the same intra- and interlingually. Source and target stand in the same theoretical relation. The spaces for potential misprision between them are, formally, identical. Thus all human beings implicated in the generation and reception of meaning are translators *even when they are strictly monoglot.* Almost paradoxically, the profusion of mutually incomprehensible tongues after Babel only dramatizes the constant differentiations and misreadings within any one language.

The obstacles posed, the theoretical and practical room for error, are such as to make of any mutual understanding, of any translation, however crass or rough-shod, something of a wonder. How is it at all possible to convey and decipher meaning, itself the most problematic of philosophic notions, across time, across space, across the more or less yawning gap between vocabularies, grammars, networks of diachronic and synchronic systems of sense which separate languages, communities, and civilizations? As I. A. Richards was fond of saying, an act of translation from classical Chinese into modern English may be the most complex process known on the planet. No translation, above the level of monosyllabic or technical tautology, is ever perfect. No understanding between speakers in the same language is perfect either. Nonetheless, the barriers to interlingual translation are or can seem so drastic as to render the labor self-defeating. There are poets and novelists and metaphysicians who have, with more or less sincere determination, condemned translation (I would cite Nabokov). In a number of religious cultures, the transfer of sacred and ritual texts into any other language is prohibited. Translation not only falsifies: it despoils the original of its numinous, secret force. Why not, in the commanding cases, make the effort to acquire the language whose "world-texts" one is intent on reading at first hand? The Greek of the New Testament is almost introductory; Virgil's Latin can be mastered (centuries of school education testify to the fact); there are those who read Dante, Lady Murasaki, or Pushkin in the original, though their own tongue is neither Italian nor Japanese nor Russian. These are reproachful, incontrovertible solicitations. They often humiliate me.

In actual fact, of course, our cultures, our histories, the minimal literacies which bind our social-ideological structures, depend on translation. Be it that of the Bible or of Roman Law; be it, across the globe, that of Shakespeare. Until the very recent planetary tide of Anglo-American English, the instruments of science and technology, of medicine and finance, of politics and trade depended on a veritable industry of translation. Parallel texts, "Rosetta stones," interlinears, translations extending over a vast gamut of possibilities, from the word-for-word primer and traveler's phrase-book to pinnacles of poetic re-creation, have kept the blood-stream of history circulating. Without translation we would inhabit parishes bordering on silence.

How, where does the human brain house language(s)? How does the cortex of the polyglot, native or by acquisition, discriminate between, keep apart different languages? (Overlaps, interference effects, confusions do tell us that this discrimination is not airtight, that it can falter under stress or with age.) Are different languages internalized at different spatial points (synapses, transformers) in the cerebral and nervous system? Is there any limit, psychologically or physiologically, to the number of different languages a man or woman can acquire (there are language-accumulators as there are virtuosi of mental arithmetic and memory)? How is "room made" for a new language in the storage and recuperation mechanisms of the cortical network? All of which are preliminary questions to that concerning the dynamics of translation, of the actual switch from one language to another – a capacity which in so-called "simultaneous translation" operates virtually instantaneously.

There are psycholinguists and neurochemists who believe that there will be material answers to these questions. They argue that the internalization and emission of language-signals will, one day, be shown to be a neurochemical, an electro-molecular sequence as, in their model, are perception and memory. Translation would then be a sub-class of the general neuro-physiology of meaning and pattern-recognitions. I am not competent to judge this prognosis. Intuition almost persuades me that it will be frustrated. The essential difficulty is that of any definition and positivist construct of consciousness itself. When, in depth, consciousness is brought to bear analytically on consciousness, the circularities are irremediable. So far, machine-translation and the electronic simulation of what are conjectured to be cerebral methods of linguistic transfer, enjoin skepticism. Mechanical translation is in essence a macro-glossary, an accelerated "looking-up" of possibly equivalent or corresponding terms in a prepared lexicon. It works, where at all, in highly specified, bounded fields: say in the perfunctory replication of a document in petroleum engineering or in some precise area (*Sprachfeld*) of commerce or finance. There is, as yet, no reliable evidence that machine-translation, however sophisticated its software, can render, even at rudimentary levels, a corpus of natural language, let alone of language with any philosophic or literary claims. In these categories, discourse, already on the scale of the single word or phrase, is formally and substantively incommensurable. There are no *a priori,* formalizable limits to the processes of motion and transformation in meaning, to the concentric spheres of implicit historical, local suggestion and connotation, to innovation (the neologism, the expansion, or contraction always latent in the known term or idiom). Language is quicksilver; it cannot be immobilized in electronic boxes. We simply do not know how the brain, how human consciousness produce articulate sense, nor how they move from one sense-code to another in translation. We can, at best, make out, via the study of cerebral lesions and speech-pathologies, something of the awesome fragility and complexity of the proceeding.

This is why I believe that "theories of translation" are an arrogant misnomer. The concept of "theory," entailing as it must that of crucial experiments and falsifications, is, as I have said, when invoked by the humanities, largely spurious. Its prestige in the current climate of humanistic-academic studies derives from an almost pitiable endeavor to ape the good fortune, the public status of the pure and applied sciences. The diagrams, the arrows with which "theoreticians" of translation adorn their proposals, are factitious. They can prove nothing. What we have to examine are accounts, discouragingly rare and fitful, which translators have left us from their work-shops. From Roman antiquity to the present, half a dozen thinkers on language and translation have made seminal suggestions. They are, for manifest reasons, hardly more numerous than those who have had anything fundamental to teach us on the meanings of music. Added to this, there is the mass of translation *per se,* circa ninety percent of which is defective or indifferently routine, but which also includes marvels of improbability. Approaches to this material and to the questions it poses are essentially intuitive and descriptive. They are narratives of patience. The rubric is, to borrow a phrase from Wittgenstein, that of an "exact art." I have tried to set out the philosophy and poetics of this art in *After Babel.* The book sought to map largely untraveled terrain. It has been honored by being pillaged and quarried since (usually without acknowledgment).

The "motion of spirit" (Dante's phrase) in translation is fourfold. Facing the text, we presume that it has meaning, however elusive or hermetic. Normally, we make this presumption unthinking. We simply postulate that the text to be translated is not non-sense, that it is not random gibberish or a one-time, unbreakable cryptogram. Axiomatically, we proceed as if there was "sense to be made" and transferred. This assumption is, in fact, audacious and charged with epistemological consequence. It is founded on the belief that semantic markers have content, that language and the world it relates and relates to are correspondently meaningful (without "black holes"). Such a belief exactly parallels that of Descartes: human reason can function only if no malign demon has muddled reality so as to deceive our senses or so as to change the rules of inference and causality in the midst of the organization, the "game," of perception and understanding. Any such operative belief or "leap of reason" in respect of the meaningfulness of words and signs, has psychological, philosophical, and ultimately theological intuitions or entailments at its roots (this is the argument at the core of *Real Presences* [1989]). These intuitions underwrite – a telling image – speech-acts and the translations which arise from them. At the immediate level, we cannot proceed without them.

After the axiomatic moment of ontological trust, comes aggression. The translator invades the original. He decomposes it into lexical, grammatical parts. This dissection comports obvious dangers. So many translations kill, literally. Imperatively, unavoidably, the translator severs the ligaments which, in any serious text, make "form" and "content" reciprocally generative and rigorously fused. Not only in the obvious case of poetry, such dissolution is, more often than not, fatal. Paradoxically, there can be fatalities and betrayals "from above." If the vast majority of translations fall short of the source-texts, there are those which surpass them, whose autonomous strength obscures and marginalizes the humbler "self" of the original. I call this betrayal "transfiguration." The high music of Rilke's *Umdichtung* all but obscures the domestic warmth and privacy of the sonnets of Louise Labé. Ortega y Gasset speaks of the "sadness of translation." Principally, he alludes to a servitude ending in inadequacy or outright failure. But there is also a *tristitia* that comes, as in eros of too violent and transforming a possession.

Thirdly, there is "home-coming," the transport of the "captured" sense back to one's native tongue and ground. It is precisely with reference to translation that St. Jerome, a formidable practitioner, speaks of meaning made captive and brought home in, as it were, a Roman triumph. Here again, the effects can be ambiguous. Tyndale's and Luther's biblical translations re-create English and German, respectively; through their versions the two languages take on their modern genius. So determinant is the imported presence ("vanquished Greece becomes Rome's teacher") that the native tongue and sensibility are profoundly altered to accommodate its arrival and incorporation. Renderings of Shakespeare have re-drawn the lineaments, the means of imagination and diction in German and in Russian. On the personal level, immersion in translation, the voyage out and back, can leave the translator unhoused. He finds himself or herself neither wholly at ease in his or her own language nor in that (in those) which he or she has mastered for translation. Walter Benjamin's image is that of a translator so possessed by metamorphosis – it is Hölderlin he had in mind – that "the doors of his own language swing shut behind him." Eminent translators have spoken of a no man's land.

The fourth motion is the crux. It is also the most difficult to put abstractly or descriptively. If it is to achieve veritable completion, the business of translation, with its invasion and acquisition of the original, must compensate. It must "make good" – a challenging idiom – its incursion, rapacity, and profit. In one respect, it does so by giving to the original a new resonance, a longer life, a wider readership, a more substantial place in history and culture. Translation is the oxygen of bounded speech-communities and neglected traditions. But the issue is subtler. Unavoidably, even the finest of translators will, as the Italian word-play insists, *traduce.* He will have curtailed, padded, embroidered, chosen limiting options in the source-text. What a truly inspired (very rare) act of translation offers in reparation is something *new that was already there.* This is not mysticism. Any thoughtful translator will know precisely what I mean. Poetry, in particular, is so manifold in its potentialities of significance and suggestion across time, is so resistant to any total anatomy or paraphrase, that it contains, in a state both latent and active (quantum), energies which the translator can elicit, release, bring into clarified play. When Valéry translates Virgil, when Leyris translates Hopkins, when Celan renders Valéry or Ungaretti, the Latin, French, or Italian texts are left, in some palpable sense, richer, more fulfilled than before. They have come into possession, perhaps for the first time, of what was already theirs. This is as near as I can come to giving "fidelity" in translation a verifiable meaning and test. Thus the fourfold proceeding from encounter, from the gamble on significance to the final act of restoration is, fundamentally, a dialectic of trust, a taking and a giving back. Where it is wholly achieved, great translations being much rarer than great literature, translation is no less than felt discourse between two human beings, ethics in action. This also is part of the harvest of Babel.

Ethnolinguists put at somewhere between 15,000 and 20,000 the number of distinct tongues once spoken on the planet. More than two-thirds have already become extinct. As I write, languages among minority cultures and in the underdeveloped world are dying out at an ever-accelerating rate. For many of these, the sole after-life is that of a tape-recording, itself fragile, of the last native speaker in some anthropological archive. The economic-technological might of Anglo-American has steamrollered across the globe. At present, it is difficult to make out any effective riposte to this detergent sovereignty. Spanish is on the march and Chinese looks to be impregnable. But even in Latin America and in China, Anglo-American is the indispensable second language and the medium of science and commerce. The thought of a more or less monoglot world is no longer inconceivable.

As I have suggested, the cost would be, is immense. Once more, a Darwinian analogy is pertinent, if native tongues were indeed to be reduced to a domestic, almost sentimental modus. Languages are being wiped out, just as are the flora and fauna of great tracts of the earth. Unnatural selection, that made by geopolitical force and ideological promise, is eliminating the numerically small and the pragmatically weak. But there is, we have seen, no such thing as a "small" language. There is no such thing as a "primitive" syntax. Each tongue, we know, generates and articulates a world-view, a narrative of human destiny, a construct of futurities for which there is no facsimile in any other. Sere is (was) spoken by a handful of villagers in the midst of a cluster of Oubangi languages. The Nigerian-Cameroon language-group includes some sixty-six distinct tongues, among them Mom (also known as Banum), with its own system of writing. Kamsa was, until recently, spoken in one lone village of eastern Columbia by the last survivors of the Mokoa people. Who is to say what Odysseys, what creation-myths, what intricacies of grammar, exploring, calling into being landscapes of sorrow or utopia, did not inhere, were not potentially present, in these several speech-worlds? What singular revelations as to social perception attach to the absence in certain Bushmen grammars of what we would designate as an accusative (*le genre objectif*)? Already, it is too late for us to be certain.

The death of a language, be it whispered by the merest handful on some parcel of condemned ground, is the death of a world. With each day, the number of different ways in which we can say "hope" diminishes. On its minute scale, my polyglot condition has been my uttermost luck. Thanks be to Babel.

8

It is plausible to suppose that the period since August 1914 has been, notably in Europe and Russia, from Madrid to Moscow, from Sicily to the Arctic Circle, the most bestial in recorded history. There are two counter-arguments.

Horror has always been endemic to the historical circumstance, to political-social realities. We know of no epoch without its massacres. Those perpetrated during, for example, the Hunnish or Tartar incursions, ran to hundreds of thousands of victims. Entire communities were extirpated. After the Thiry Years' War, wolves ran free in the burnt, empty hamlets and towns of the principalities of Germany and Central Europe. Historians vary in their estimates of the numbers done to death in such cleansings of heresy as the Albigensian Crusade, or of those tortured and executed during successive witch-crazes. But they were high. The Black Death was only one in a long sequence of epidemics which left devastating demographic damage. From the time of ancient Rome onward, judicial torture and the enslavement of the conquered, under diverse categories of serfdom and servitude, have been perennial. Of comparable weight, albeit less visible, less graphically documented, is the *misère* of the daily life for the non-privileged, for the actual mass of men and women in the peasantry and laboring classes. Recurrently, millions have subsisted on the constant edge of hunger, in habitations unfit even for animals, in illiteracy and a more or less conscious acceptance of disease, infant mortality, humiliation, and early death. Almost to the present, the chronicle of European and Russian women (not to speak of the "Third World") outside a chosen circle of good fortune, has been that of more or less brutal victimization. For the vast majority of human beings, childhood meant a zone of darkness. Only occasionally does recorded history throw any light on the deprivations, on the undernourishment of body and mind, on the brutalization suffered by children, so many dying young, in the hovels of the medieval or Victorian slum, on land owned by exploiting masters or in the mines and factories of the industrial revolution. European, Russian acres have been, quite literally, blood-drenched or drenched with sweat since the Dark Ages. Killing-fields have followed on killing-fields. No period can boast of any novel or crowning inhumanity.

The second argument, which relates to the misery of common man over these millennia, directs us to the advances in technology and the sciences in the twentieth century. Ninety percent of all scientists are now living. The period, roughly, since Darwin, Rutherford, and Einstein has seen an exponential flowering of fundamental and applied science. Our understanding of the cosmos, of evolution, of the neurophysiology of the human species, has been enriched a hundredfold. To Archimedes and Galileo, but even to Newton and to Gauss, much of what a schoolchild is today expected to master would have been totally inaccessible. This is the century of Dirac. The bio-genetics, the molecular biology which follow on the mapping of DNA are revolutionizing basic concepts of human potentiality. The image of man is changing. Horizons seem to accelerate before us towards an ever more complex and challenging light.

In turn, the transformations of individual and social conditions fueled by science and its practical applications are far greater than throughout the entirety of preceding history. At decisive points of health, information, and communication, men and women of the mid-eighteenth century were closer to ancient Athens than we are to them. The gains achieved in medicine have transmuted the history of pain. As C. S. Lewis used to remind his students: "Shut your eyes for a moment and picture life before chloroform." Health-care has altered time in regard to early mortality and life-expectations. "Genetic engineering" may soon redraft the human blueprint. Our daily time and space are no longer those of Kant or even of Edison. Instantaneities of communication, the overpowering *accelerando* of global travel, touch, will touch on almost every nerve of human awareness and habit. Communication has become our fourth dimension. And although there are apparently cyclical hiccups in the economic system, and although vast tracts of poverty, hunger, and disease remain to be eradicated in the underdeveloped regions, a general, indeed dramatic amelioration in the quality of human existence is evident. Unprecedented resources, comforts, and opportunities are either available or in prospect. The escalator of life runs upward.

Both of these counter-statements against pessimism carry obvious weight. It would be fatuous to leave them out of account. Or to make any facile use of the paradox whereby these scientific-technical advances entail misuse (e.g., nuclear arsenals, the threat of a politics of genetic planning and cloning). Undeniably, history has always been a witches' Sabbath, and, at numerous psychological and material points, many of us "have never had it so good." Amen.

Nonetheless, the case for a recognition of our age as most probably the blackest is strong. Statistics are vital, but they mock the imagination. We cannot take in the figures. Conservative estimates put at circa *75 million* the total of men, women, and children gunned, bombed, gassed, starved to death, slaughtered during deportations, slave-labor, and famines between 1914 and the closure of the Gulags (roughly nine million perished amid cannibalism and suicide during Stalin's elimination of the Kulaks in the Ukraine). Five British infantrymen died every fifty seconds during the first days on the Somme. Historians gauge at half a million the corpses left to rot or to be pounded into mud in front of Verdun. Like the Weimar monetary collapse – a billion Marks for a loaf of bread – the hecatombs of the First World War undermined the conceptual reality of large numbers. It is a matter of macabre semantics, offensive to reason, to try and determine whether or not, and in what ways, the Shoah, the Holocaust is unique; whether or not it defines a singularity in the history of mankind. Perhaps it does. Perhaps there is no other instance, precisely analogous of ontological massacre – this is to say, of the deliberate murder of human beings whose guilt, minutely verbalized and set out by bureaucracy, was that of *being*. The millions of Jews beaten, burnt, tortured, marched, starved, gassed to extinction, the men and women drowned in cess-pits, the children thrown alive into fire, the old men hanged on meat-hooks, had committed the sole crime of existing. Even the fetus had to be torn out of the womb, lest there be even one Jew left to bear witness, to remember (though no one would believe him or her, a point the Nazis made with derisive logic). Are the Armenian massacres, the genocide in Rwanda analogous? I do not know. What I do know is that the unspeakable technology of humiliation, torture, and butchery – merely to cite them is to scar and in some sense dehumanize language, as I tried to show in *Language and Silence* (1967) – arising out of an unresolved demonology and, it may be, self-hatred in European Christendom, created on this earth a material mirror-image of imagined Hell. Time and space were made static eternities of suffering in what the Nazis, unconsciously echoing Dante, called "the anus of the world" (Auschwitz).

Simultaneously, and for decades thereafter, Stalinism consigned its millions (seven, ten, fifteen?) to living burial in the mines of Kolyma, to planned starvation, to slow death by freezing and forced labor. It is said that the despot, during the blood-carnival of the great purges, signed up to 2,000 death-warrants *per diem,* sentences which meant the annihilation of whole families, the confinement of young children in state orphanages, the eradication of ethnic cultures.

Nor has the sequence of mass-murder on tribal, ideological, or political grounds ceased. Half a million in Indonesia; as many in Burundi. It is now thought, in sober analysis, that approximately 100,000 men, women, children were *buried alive* – should one write, let alone try to attach concrete meaning to such a sentence? – in the killing-fields of Cambodia by the Khmer Rouge. As I write, mass-graves of the clubbed to death, of the raped are turning up in Bosnia and Croatia. How many millions are, this day, at slave-labor in Chinese "re-education" camps or in Burmese prisons? The winds of mass-homicide, of "ethnic cleansing," of fundamentalist hatreds blow over Gaza, over Africa. Amnesty International indexes more than one hundred nations (which include Israel and Britain in Northern Ireland) at whose behest torture is an accepted practice. The systematic economic and sexual abuse of children is thought, by qualified observers, to be at its highest level in human history (the number of children in "slave-factories" or on serf-farms is put at 200 million). Thus the inventory of the inhuman continues without end.

Do we know this because, like never before, we are informed, because the news-media bombard us with daily revelations? In earlier epochs, horrors could escape notice or be noised abroad only gradually and diffusely. No doubt, this is a telling factor. But one that cuts both ways. Our very awareness of what man is inflicting on man should trigger outrage and intervention (the media kept the world informed of the savageries of Mao's Cultural Revolution, of the insane sadism of Pol Pot). Almost invariably, however, the frequency, the packaged unreality of media presentation leaves us either numbed or rapidly forgetful. Massacres, documentaries of torture and genocide, flash across our screens with ephemeral routine. We opt out of the unbearable, vaguely reassured, even absolved by the pathos of knowing.

Yet should we not be immensely astonished?

The Enlightenment, voices as clairvoyant as Voltaire's and Jefferson's, had proclaimed an end to judicial torture, to the burning of dissenters and of books. The abolition of slavery was imminent. Nineteenth-century positivism and a spectrum of liberal and of socialist-messianic programs, Marxism foremost among them, had envisioned mankind on a long, sometimes tortuous, but inherently certain march towards political emancipation, social justice, economic well-being, and peace (whose universality Kant had deemed a realistic concept). Overall, Europe and even Russia had avoided all but a handful of "professional" and localized wars between Waterloo and 1914. These are the one hundred years of progress, of liberal-bourgeois flowering, with their (relative) safety in the streets, with their (relative) freedom of belief, speech, and inquiry on which we now look back with unnerved nostalgia. Concomitantly, science and technology made such advances as to induce, reasonably, the expectation that the developed nations and the worlds overseas to whom such progress must, inevitably, extend, would no longer yield to mass-hysteria, to lunatic creeds, to

tribal blood-lust. Again, the ironies now come close to being unbearable. The orgy of armaments is today very largely out of control. It keeps industrial and underdeveloped economies locked in
mutual corruption. Science is often helpless before misuse. Sophisticated antibiotics were applied in Argentine torture-cells to
keep the "patient" alive for the next session. Religious fundamentalism rages. Ethnic loathings have rarely been more murderous.
These are our icons for the close of the millennium.

The facts of Auschwitz and of Hiroshima, the abolition in
warfare of any discrimination between civilian and military, the
slaughter (often planned) of women and children, may prove to be
irreparable. They will have marked, at depths of consciousness
and self-consciousness all but inaccessible to repair, both victim
and killer, both the torturer and the tortured. In a dialectic analogous to that on Golgotha, the Jew occasioned and released the
bestial in other men (Germans were not the only ones at work).
The camp-guard, the terrorist, the torturer, the killer-gangs in our
inner cities, the apologist for racism and political-religious madness, wherever he operates – from Guatemala to Siberia, from
Rwanda to Belsen – makes something less than human both of his
victims and himself. Thus it is, I believe, difficult to deny that the
twentieth century has lowered the threshold of humanity. Man
has, on a pervasive scale, been diminished.

This belief governs my politics. Where, however, "politics" is too
pretentious a word. It implies a coherent investment in ideology, in
party, in process which I have not mustered. "Political intuitions,"
"contradictory reflexes" would be more appropriate. It is undeniable that human beings – how many, for what motives? – are
capable of altruism, of active compassion, of self-sacrifice to the
point of death. There are men and women possessed in spirit and
body by empathy for others, by love of infirm humanity, by a

radiant thirst for justice. Every night of the year there are those who
serve in geriatric wards, nursing, easing into release the inconti-
nent, the palsied, the deranged. Children hideously handicapped
and without hope of normalcy are cared for, are vehemently loved
also by those not kindred to them. A very few – half a dozen out of
six million? – took the place of others in the gas-ovens. At any given
time, the sum of everyday humaneness, of applied love, can be
considerable, and more often than not, anonymous.

On the other hand, the potentialities for, the enactments of
evil look to be perennially unbounded. The cruelties, mental and
bodily, exercised towards one's immediate kin, the abuse, fitful or
systematic, of women and children, the torment and humiliation
of animals, permeate existence like an intractable stench. Psychological "triggers," mimetic impulses, much studied but little understood, can provoke in otherwise ordinary individuals spasms of
utter sadism. These can rapidly grow habitual. Killing and torture,
the abjection of fellow human beings can become a rapidly ac-
quired taste. Even though they were at risk of no retribution if they
refused or abstained, great numbers of German men and women
turned bestial, inventing, on their own initiative, and when the
war was clearly lost, novel modes of derision and torture for their
Jewish victims. Nor is there much evidence that other nations or
ethnic communities would not, given the informing context of
collective purpose, act otherwise. So far as we know, the human
psyche in which *libido,* in which erotic-sexual desires and fantasies
do not comprise sadistic and masochistic elements, do not contain
sharp splinters of savagery, is exceptional. A primordial ferocity
lies close to desire, and even to love.

It is some such scarcely measurable (dis)equilibrium between
decency and cruelty, between moral excellence and brute animality,
which is the raw material of any social-political order. Mammals

capable of achieving high levels of ethical insight and creativity, but persistently territorial, aggressive towards competitors, prone to infection by mass-hatreds, by homicidal herd-reflexes, are required to devise institutions of civility, of self-restraint and altruistic collaboration in the *polis,* in the crowded "city of men." Little wonder that political history and social systems are susceptible to recurrent catastrophe.

After the Enlightenment and 1789, though this is an over-simplification, North American and western European political forms are meant to realize, to make dynamic a general axiom of human equality before the law, of religious-racial-ideological tolerance. They are meant to institutionalize an equitable distribution of material resources and opportunities. A presumption of equal worth attaches to each and every individual life, however humble its provenance or probable potential.

We know how slow, how labored a road led to this creed. Which is grounded in the secularization, during the seventeenth century and its scientific revolutions, of the postulate of infinite personal worth in Judeo-Christian anthropology. Which is anchored in the enigmatic dictum of man's creation in God's image. The liberal *credo* also arches back to highly selective readings of Athenian political ideals (not practice) and of Roman Law, itself so imperceptive of women, children, and slaves. Freedom of discourse, parliamentary institutions, legality, the American Supreme Court *par excellence,* embody the relevant hopes and criteria. The rhetoric which enshrines Anglo-American and west-European democratic promises has become so pervasive, so instinct with positive valuations, that we rarely pause to observe its particularity and "locality." For the vast majority of mankind, both in historical time and geographical space, modes of representative, parliamentary government, the rule of law, and the predicate of human equality in political and legal affairs have been all but irrelevant. The record of nations, societies, cultures throughout Russia, Asia, Africa has, with brief exceptions, been that of varying orders of theocratic, dictatorial, paramilitary, or clannish power-relations. The planet at large has never, until very recently, looked to what might be called in shorthand the Periclean, Jeffersonian, or liberal-progressive program for man and *communitas*. Nor has it accorded either credence or substance to the dogma of human equality be-fore the face of power. In essence, the realities of social-economic relations and daily life have been those set out by Hegel in his parable of "Master and Slave."

Human beings can be regarded as biologically equal (yet what of hereditary diseases?). We all breathe oxygen, defecate, and die – though no death is altogether like any other. This is a truth both essential and trivial. At any more developed level, the theorem of equality becomes elusive. The range of differences in human gifts, in our mental and physical capacities, is extensive. No social psy-chology, no "biometrics" can classify the manifold gaps or nuances which separate genius from the moronic, which distance the cre-ativity, the innovative energies of the few from the passivity of the many. There is, unquestionably, a sense in which a Bach, an Ein-stein, or a Mandela are the same as the child-molester or the cretin. But it is, outside the domain of theology, a sense infinitely banal. Only the invocation of God or the exercise of sainthood can perceive the distinctions but deny their weight and existential consequence. Deprivation, impotence indeed sanctify the mind-less, the most humble.

Secular democracy has to blur the issue. It cannot negate the facts of inequality, but aims to correct them through care and education. It seeks to eliminate, so far as is possible, what role they might play in the allocation of essential resources or in the face of the law. Liberal meliorism gambles on the potentiality of mental and bodily improvement in everyone. So that this potentiality should not be overlooked or wasted, the disadvantaged are to be safeguarded and furthered. In the open market-place, social "engineering" and constructive compassion are to attenuate the privileges of talent and inherited luck. In theory, moreover, the vote does make all men and women, all women and men equal. It permits Presidents of the United States to be elected by less than a third of the suffrage and licenses forty-four percent of voters to carry National Socialism to power in the Germany of the 1930s. In both theory and *praxis*, parliamentary democracy is persistently vulnerable.

We noted that the "language-animal" is equipped to act with eminent courage, altruism, and caring. He is equally, if not more so, prone to savagery, egotism, territorial appetites, and irrationalism of every kind. His/her proclivity to intellectual sloth and material greed seems boundless. This bizarre biped will destroy for the sake of destruction. Witness the barbarian hordes at one extreme, the vandals in our streets at the other. Man takes to sadism with perplexing relish. Yet this same species has developed a number of passions, of crafts of the spirit, wholly disinterested. Pure mathematics, music, poetry, philosophic speculation, certain modes of art, are disinterested. They exist, magnificently, without use. They do not, save in some metaphoric sense – metaphor being itself something of a crucial riddle – nourish or preserve biosocial survival. Only a loaded rhetoric can claim that these pure proceedings assist Darwinian goals or pacify the world. W. H. Auden was inclined to remark that poems "make nothing happen." As often, throughout this memoir, I urge amazement.

Theories of evolution, of socio-economic history, cannot account on any adaptive or utilitarian basis for the inception and flowering in the hominid brain of, say, algebraic topology or the theory of transfinite numbers. They tell us virtually nothing of the genesis of absolute music – this is to say, of music which does not mime, however indirectly, either natural or animal sounds and signals. Why do we compose lyric verse or critiques of pure judgment? To answer that such autonomous speculative ("mirroring") exercises bring us pleasure is to evade the question. Other pleasures, those of sex, food, wealth, power lie so much nearer to hand, are so much easier to come by. Long before and after Empedocles or Archimedes, men have sacrificed their lives in pursuit of a mathematical proof or a metaphysical argument. Untold personal destitution, ridicule, isolation, obscurity, not to speak of persecution on ideological-political grounds, has attended on the production of great art, literature, or philosophic investigation. We may be guilty of romanticizing our images of a Spinoza, a Schubert, or a Van Gogh – but the evidence of suffering and solitude remains overwhelming. In the midst of the inhumanity and indifference of history, a handful of men and women have been creatively possessed by the compelling splendor of the useless (the Socratic *daimonion*). This constitutes the eminent dignity, the "princeliness" of our brutal kind. It may just be that together with the saints, religious or secular, this "pride" of mathematicians, composers, poets, painters, logicians, or epistemologists (the inquirers into inquiry) in some manner ransom mankind. I am haunted by the possibility that the generation out of our mammalian midst of a Plato, a Gauss, or a Mozart justifies, redeems the species which devised and carried out Auschwitz.

What produces these magnitudes, these *novae* exploding, as it were, out of the great dust-clouds of human mediocrity? The question has been posed since the pre-Socratics. It lies at the heart of any democratic theory and model of education. Central to it is the debate over inheritance and environment, over the genetic and the social. Which part of the seminal equation is which? When it is surely obvious that these two categories are critically meshed. Genes, physiological-physical inheritance or accident *are* environment. A child born blind will not develop into a major painter. A child born out of generations of malnutrition or born into a malarial hovel, is "fated" by an inherited environment, by environmental "bio-constraints." The truth is one of indissociable interaction. Biology is environment; environment is biology. It is condescending cant to suppose otherwise.

Far more resistant is the question of the light-burst of creative capacities where conditions of material well-being are more or less current (as in the industrial, scientifically developed world). Can further improvements in the social-economic milieu – the eradication of slums, of sub-literacy, of racial and gender prejudice – raise the level, the statistical incidence of intellectual, artistic performance? The finding must be positive. Given mental stimulus, afforded vital space in which to grow and experiment, children, hitherto expended, will reach outward and imagine fruitfully. The general level of humane fulfillment is certain to rise.

What remains vexingly unclear is whether or not such overall progress relates to creativity of the first order. Mathematical insights, musical genius, the ability to draw and paint breath-takingly can, indeed do, spring out of social misery and social isolation (e.g., Giotto, the "lone shepherd-boy"). Moreover, at any given point in time and place, the statistical "scattering," the distribution of excellence in relation to the norm, looks to be tenaciously, mysteriously inelastic. If a Platonic despot chose to enforce violin lessons for all, the number of Heifetzes *might* marginally increase. Not, I believe, that of Haydns or Bartoks. First-rank aesthetic, philosophic, scientific creation seems to arise from, to inhabit its singular inward environment in unpredictable dissent from the commonplace (this is also true of chess). Its genesis, its infrequency remains "an irrational number."

But what of the consumers? Of those who are invited to hear the music, read the book, or follow the philosophic debate? One must assume that improved schooling, an increase in genuine literacy and numeracy, will widen the number of those throughout the community respondent to thought, to the arts, to literature. It will multiply "respondents." This is the impetus of the liberal pedagogy of the Enlightenment, of a Jefferson, a Matthew Arnold, an F. R. Leavis (or of my son David's book on education for responsible citizenship in a multiracial, American body politic). What evidence is there that this ideal can be attained on anything but a limited scale? Doubtless, there are bracing symptoms. Museums are fuller, classical music and jazz are reaching wider and wider audiences. Horizons of enhanced perception via the new electronic media – the CD-ROM, the Internet, Virtual Reality – are theoretically almost without limit. "High culture," responsive perception and engagement in quality, can be rendered invitingly accessible as never before. As yet, nevertheless, the compass and efficacy of the process remain questionable. The self-same media can further trivialize both knowledge and experience, meaning and form. The cyber-net can be packed with trash and incitement. It can drug sensibility to the point of inertia (the "couch-potato" in front of day-long television).

In late capitalism, money bellows. It packages time and space. The censorship of the market over what is difficult and innovative, over what is intellectually and aesthetically demanding – the "little magazine," the philosophic treatise, the *avant-garde* composition – is often more effective than that exercised by political censorship and suppression. Serious literature, music, and thought have the exasperating habit of being productive under tyranny. "Squeeze us, we are olives," said James Joyce. "Censorship is the mother of metaphor," added Borges. The mass-consumer market, the mass-media can bury alive. Freedom and license can bestow insignificance (what poem could have shaken the White House as Mandelstam's epigram shook Stalin?).

But the conundrum of inelasticity in the number and quality of respondents, despite enrichments in schooling and access, could lie deeper. It may be that the human capacity to be interested in, to be moved by, to grasp and answer to major thought and form, though self-evidently far more widespread than are the springs of creation, is itself confined to a more or less constant minority. "The truth has always been with the few" (Goethe). Education, should it purpose to do so, can enlarge this minority. But not indefinitely; not, one intuits, by very much. Men and women who desire to resolve non-linear equations, who can take in, at any coherent level, a Bach partita, who respond to a poem by Donne or seek to grapple with what Kant calls a "transcendental deduction" – each of these being among the unprofitable summits of the human story – are, will most likely continue to be, few. They are an elite. This word has been incessantly thrust at me. Yet its meaning is perfectly straightforward. An elite in the world of pop-music, of athletics, of the bourse, or of the life of the mind is simply that group which knows, which says that some things are better, are more worth getting to know and to love, than others.

It follows from this view of things that an optimal social-political regime is one which identifies, as early as possible, incipient intellectual, scientific, artistic creativity, whatever its ethnic-economic background; which then fosters such creativity by every available educational means; and which, thereafter, guarantees to the thinker or artist or scientist or writer, however anarchic his stance, however critical his dissent, psychological and material spaces in which to exercise his or her gifts. Such a regime will honor and reward true teachers almost to excess. It will, if necessary, circumscribe zones of silence, of insured privacy around the poet or logician or composer (as did the civic authorities in Jerusalem around the house of the writer, Agnon!). It will, in short, aim to elicit and cultivate a meritocracy of the unpredictable, founded on the conviction that the *dignitas,* the validation of our species on this planet, consists in the disinterested advances out of animality made by the creative spirit.

Programs for the early spotting and nurture of athletic prowess have been in force in a number of political societies. The steepening pyramid of elite *lycées* and *Grandes écoles* in France has, since Napoleon, given a deliberate, public eminence and recompense to intellectual excellence. In Ireland today, literature and the arts are afforded fiscal and social welcome and breathing-space by virtue of official largesse. The possibilities for the Platonic are there in any advanced community. But not, on the whole, the political consensus. Certainly not in mass-consumption and egalitarian democracies.

Quite obviously, the Periclean-Florentine model I have in mind – was it ever, in fact, realized? – will strike the vast majority of "normal" citizens as absurd and even offensive. It speaks of and for a minority, an "aristocracy" worse than hereditary. It patronizes common humanity and, perhaps, common sense. The (sad) fact is that ninety-five percent or more of mankind does get along more or less satisfactorily or grimly, as the case may be, without the slightest interest in Bach fugues, in Immanuel Kant's synthetic *a priori,* or Fermat's last theorem (whose recent solution is a point of light in the tawdriness of the closing century). Immured in the daily treadmill of material survival, in child-bearing and rearing, the "commonwealth" of man takes these matters, where it has any awareness of them whatsoever, to be more or less otiose games, demonstrably luxurious and too often irresponsible or devilish in their consequences. Hence the counter-icons of the mad scientist, of the deranged artist, of the metaphysician falling in the well. It remains incontrovertible that for close to the totality of *homo sapiens sapiens* the current world-faith is that of football. Tea-dance tunes or rock exalt, move, console hundreds of millions for whom a Beethoven sonata would spell boredom. Given a free vote, the thousand-fold plurality of my fellow human beings will elect a television soap or quiz-show over Aeschylus, will choose bingo over chess. And it is just this freedom of choice, even where the options are pre-selected and pre-packaged by the economic domi-nance of the media and mass-market, which is fundamentally consonant with the ideals and the institutions of democracy.

Moreover: what right has the mandarin to enforce "high" cul-ture? What license has the pedagogue or so-called intellectual to cram his esoteric priorities and values down the throats of what Shakespeare called "the general" (i.e., those averse to caviar)? The more so if and when he knows, in his troubled heart of hearts, that intellectual and artistic achievements do not seem to render men and society more humane, more apt for justice and mercy? When he intuits that the humanities do not humanize, that the sciences, and even philosophy can serve the worst of politics? (I have ad-dressed much of my own life and work to this bleak paradox.) What justification have I, outside personal taste or vanity, to op-pose, like Quixote and his windmills, popular culture and what it so manifestly contributes to lives otherwise drab or crippled? On any pragmatic-democratic basis, on that of social justice, the an-swer is: none.

Coercion on behalf of the "classic" in the arts, music, and

literature can be exercised by despotic regimes. Such enforcement did produce certain remarkable results in the Soviet Union and pre-1989 eastern Europe. At certain times, in East Berlin or Warsaw or Leningrad, it may have looked as if Goethe and Schiller, Mozart and Pushkin had eclipsed trash. I recall evenings in Berlin with half a dozen classical-musical recitals and serious plays, ranging from Sophocles to Shakespeare and Brecht, on offer. I plead guilty to finding this somewhat grimly intoxicating. The concomitant price of oppression, of censorship was, to be sure, intolerable. The pedagogic impact, moreover, appears to have been short-lived. In the book-stores I knew in East Berlin or in Weimar, where they have survived at all, Jackie Collins and the video-cassette have swiftly ousted Lessing and Hölderlin. Virtually overnight, freedom reclaimed its inalienable right to junk-food.

I repeat: these truths and arguments are irrefutable. They breathe the air of democracy. They are, at the same time, impertinent – in the etymological sense – to my *credo* and the options which it imposes. Any attempt at serious thought, be it mathematical, scientific, metaphysical, or formal, in the widest creative-poetic vein, is a vocation. It comes to possess one like an unbidden, often unwelcome summons. Even the teacher, the expositor, the critic who lacks creative genius but who devotes his existence to the presentment and perpetuation of the real thing, is a being infected (*krank an Gott*). Pure thought, the analytic compulsion, the *libido sciendi* which drive consciousness and reflection towards abstraction, towards aloneness and heresy, are cancers of the spirit. They grow, they may devour the tissues of normalcy in their path. But cancers are non-negotiable. This is the point.

I have no sound leg to stand on if I try to apologize for the social cost of, say, grand opera in a context of slums and destitute hospitals. I can never prove that Archimedes was right to sacrifice his life to a problem in the geometry of conic sections. It happens to be blindingly obvious to me that study, theological-philosophic argument, classical music, poetry, art, all that is "difficult because it is excellent" (Spinoza, patron-saint of the possessed) are the excuse for life. I am convinced that one is infinitely privileged to be even a secondary attendant, commentator, instructor, or custodian in some reach of these high places. I cannot, I must not negotiate this passion. Such negotiation, of which "political correctness" is an infantile, deeply mendacious tactic, is the treason of the cleric. It is, as in the unreason of love, a lie.

Barring a republic of excellence, the social contract should, so far as I can make out, reduce, among its participants, the aggregate of pain and of hatred. Our communal and international relations are awash with both. Totalitarian (Hegelian) systems conscript hatred and institutionalize pain. They marshal, they direct them towards the internal scapegoat and the foreign foe. Bureaucracies of menace and abjection use pain at every level. The police-states in Africa, Latin America, and the Middle East, the concentration camps and the Gulag, "re-education" in China or Burma, are functional rationalizations of both hatred and pain. The social order depends on the fact that these two instruments are a state monopoly. Open and democratic societies are therapeutic. They endeavor to alleviate pain and lessen hatred. For the latter in particular they seek to provide relatively innocuous channels and surrogates. Licensed aggression in the free market and in sports are a paramount example. Fictive violence is richly available. From early childhood onward, those addicted to television, notably in North America and western Europe, will have witnessed thousands of hours of homicide, assault, rape, humiliation. The spiral of graphic brutality in the media, on the Internet, may now be spinning out of control. In the United States, women's wrestling is a rapidly growing spectator sport. The sources of this voracity for violence, for the mimed infliction of pain in even the most democratic, materially privileged social systems remain unclear. It is conceivable that there fester, notably but by no means exclusively, in the male of the species biosomatic atavisms of aggression (of territorial "road rage"). Ritual, symbolic warfare, like that of the urban street-gangs or contact-sports, no longer feeds the appetite which, like a muffled earth-tremor, pulses within the psyche after too prolonged a period of peace (since 1945). As has often been noted, today's football hooligan would excel as tomorrow's commando.

As I write, there are near to thirty million jobless in industrial Europe. No doubt, the economy will right itself, but emerging patterns of manpower-minimal automation and technocracy suggest that a considerable proportion of young people will never qualify for normal, long-range employment, let alone job-security. At a more drastic pitch, poverty and ethnic divisions throughout the Balkans, the Arab sphere, or the patchwork-quilt of African tribalism, leave a growing number of men and women wasted. What have they to look forward to? A Kalashnikov automatic rifle, a machete, have become for millions the emblem of virility, of self-assertion, of possible reward.

It is by no means certain that parliamentary democracy, in contexts of racial stress and economic cycles, can contain, not to say dissipate the prodigalities of violence. Classic liberal equations between democratic institutions and economic progress are unraveling (cf. the economies of southeast Asian military or semi-military oligarchies). There are not many urban communities more plagued by violence than Los Angeles in the midst of explosive economic development. Only one thing seems clear: the sheer irrelevance to much, to most of the over-populated and famished earth of Anglo-American ideals of the rule of law and the parliamentary process. If asked to choose between these exalted principles and economic security, between the freedom to publish – how many men or women write books, how many read them? – and protection from pauperization in old age, between a plurality of political parties and safety or hygiene in their streets, millions will opt for the latter.

Despite the detergent ubiquity of the planetary media, differences remain profound. Fundamentalism, that blind lunge towards simplification, towards the infantile comforts of imposed discipline, is immensely on the march. In regard to Islam, European democracies stand increasingly bewildered and vulnerable. Prognostication is usually specious. It does look possible, however, that the coming centuries will witness fierce conflicts between irreconcilable cultures, between antithetical world-visions even more divided by mutual fears and hatreds than are the ideological and ethnic camps of today.

In the nascent American republic, Thoreau found most of his fellow citizens living lives "of quiet desperation." Today, these desperations grow raucous and impatient. I have had neither the compulsion nor the courage to enter politics. In Aristotelian terms, such abstention amounts to idiocy. It gives to the thugs, the corrupt, and the mediocre every incentive and opportunity to take over. The sum of my politics is to try and support whatever social order is capable of reducing, even marginally, the aggregate of hatred and of pain in the human circumstance. And which allows privacy and excellence breathing-space. I think of myself as a Platonic anarchist. Not, I realize, a winning ticket.

9

I have been lucky in my teachers. They left me persuaded that, at its best, the relation of teacher to student is an enacted allegory of disinterested love.

I have said something of the pressure-cooker ambience, pedagogic and political, which prevailed at the French *Lycée* in Manhattan during the war. Three of us chose the "classical" option for the baccalaureat. This meant learning ancient Greek. Once weekly, we were delivered into the hands of Jean Boorsch. He traveled down from Yale where he taught French Literature. This alone imbued him with an aura of magisterial authority. Boorsch was not a physically prepotent or robust figure. But he was made coldly luminous and intense by a singular blend of irony and elevation. He possessed mesmeric eyes and a trick of the mouth signifying caustic sadness at our efforts. The resistant marvels of Greek syntax and style filled him with visible content. The two hours under his ferule were an *agon*, a *polemos*, a match for survival. It soon dawned on the two of us who stayed the course that this didactic method, this elegant violence in instruction, itself mirrored the conflictual *élan*, the menace of dialogue and dialectic which energize the Greek language and the Attic spirit from Pindar to Plutarch.

Like all eminent pedagogues, Boorsch, as he darted to and fro or turned on us, became the "figuration," the presence made visible of his theme. He immersed us in the three surviving orations of Andocides, a rebarbative rhetorician-advocate of the fourth century B.C. When my companion and I finally dared query – could Monsieur Boorsch not lead us to greener pastures, to Demosthenes, say, or the poets? – the retort was withering. Any fool could take delight in and chatter about manifest eloquence and lyricism. It was precisely a mediocre exemplar, a precisian in shades of gray, who would lay bare the sinews of grammar, the rhetorical resources of ancient Greek *per se*. So Andocides it was, and his uncompromising cunning, according to Boorsch, in the deployment, for our aching benefit, of irregular verbs.

Boorsch's spell extended beyond the class-room. He had, in France, been in the cavalry. His peremptory demands, the rigid glance derived (or so we romanced) from the celebrated *manège* and tactics of the Saumur cavalry school. We were heirs to that *dressage*. Nor was our halting pursuit of the Greek aorist and optative the sole spur to Boorsch's hebdomadal raid on New York. When he strode out of our lives and *Lycée* on those Thursday afternoons, he did not head directly back to Yale. We had unearthed (I do not recall exactly how) a clandestine liaison. There was a mistress to whom, we excitedly fancied, he would, amid sexual gallantries, reveal the absurdities and occasional brilliance of his two disciples. The harsh, inspired teacher, the ex-cavalry officer, the secret amorist: it was only years later that I came across Jean Boorsch's pioneering study of Descartes's readings of Montaigne. He had never alluded to it, though he knew, dismissively, of my enthusiasms. His was an arrogance of reserve, a passing of fastidious judgment on what he took to be his limitations.

Jean Boorsch initiated me, made me responsive to, the magnetism of philology. It is in the minutiae, in the arcane irregularities of grammar that we can observe the immediacies of intuition, the incipience of thought and style pressing, like hot metal, on the mold of articulation. Syntax, the temporalities informing and informed by verb-tenses, the conventions of predication and nomination proper to a given tongue or epoch, are the nerve-structure of feeling and of argument. Moreover, outwardly dry, even spinsterish, philological studies are inhabited by a peculiar violence. We see this in Lorenzo Valla, stabbed for his editorial pains, in Housman's reviews and emendations, in Nabokov at play on textual cruces in Pushkin. Philological controversies can breed pure and lasting hatreds. Polemics between lexicographers or grammarians exhibit an *odium* as vehement, as personalized as that attributed to theologians (the two vocations are kindred). In the master-grammarian, in the ranking textual scholar and editor, technicality becomes interpretative vision. The thicket, the underbrush of minute detail, of etymological dissection, of emendation opens on to a clearing of responsible, respondent perception. I am thinking of William Empson on the word "fool" in *Lear;* of Gianfranco Contini on dialect and vulgate in the *Commedia.* At some rudimentary level, I garnered from M. Boorsch and the wretched parsing of Andocides a glimpse of that promised land. I sensed the mustard-seed of love (*philein*) in philology, perhaps even in logic, itself, for so much of Western history, indivisible from rhetoric. I have lacked the tenacity, the patience needed to follow on. In her studies of ancient Greek poetry and rhetorical modes, my daughter, Deborah, has done so. Boorsch would have approved of her.

My failings must have been utterly visible to Ernest Sirluck when he handed back to me my first essay for his Milton seminar marked, tersely, "Flamboyant." A marmoreal verdict. Sirluck was new to the University of Chicago. He had come from Toronto and war-service. Like many young instructors in a somewhat awesome academic setting, he sought assurance in a persona: that of the almost Victorian scholar-moralist, unsparing in his professional criteria, contemptuous of hedonism and any signs of dalliance in one's work. His lapidary concision, his insistence on the authority of his views, the excessive work-load he imposed on his students – a symptom of inexperience – bred a small but devoted following. As in the case of Jean Boorsch, one took pride in survival, not to speak of severely rationed commendations. The pass-words were "severity," "rigor," and "scruple." Applied to Milton, and particularly to the radical Latinity of Milton's theological-political prose, they produced formidable clarities. At a time when literary studies at Chicago veered between a neo-Aristotelian formalism and the impact of the New Criticism – the poem as autonomous object – Ernest Sirluck (the name was emblematic of the man) drilled his students in historical context, linguistic history, rhetoric, and the awareness of Renaissance and Puritan ideologies. His contempt for editorial ignorance or "free-floating" aesthetics (i.e., chit-chat among those unable to muster a Latin declension) was barbed. He was, though unaware of the fact, closer than anyone I had come up against previously, to the historicism, to the ethical-political bent of the best of Marxist literary theory.

I do not recall at precisely which point the troubled privacy, the vulnerability under the armored surface, came through to me. Perhaps during a penetrative class on Milton's Hebraism. I ought to have known at once that Ernest Sirluck was a Jew and that his proud defensiveness arose out of this condition. Which was to determine also, as his autobiography, *First Generation* (1996) sets out, the subsequent vicissitudes of his academic-administrative career in Canada. Too many fellow teachers, deans, politicians, and I dare say, students have let Sirluck down. They have fallen short either of the professional rigor or of the moral clarity which learning and the ideals of a university should command. I did not become the textual-historical scholar Sirluck expected. I can only

guess uneasily at what he makes of my work and of any light it may
throw on his own abstention from producing the corpus to which
his gifts and passions directed him. We have become friends.
When my books are not what they should be, I hear his pained
voice.

To read the *Nichomachean Ethics* under Richard McKeon's
guidance was a privilege. He was neither a classicist nor an analyst
of ancient philosophy of the first rank (cf. Leo Strauss). But he
brought to Aristotle a twofold insight. That of the Thomist, subtly
at home in the Scholastic uses of the ancient texts and in the
extraordinary role which these uses play in Western intellectual
and political affairs. Secondly, McKeon was a public man, a nota-
ble influence in American cultural polices and UNESCO. This stiff-
ened his commentary on Aristotle with the weight, with the pragmatic constraints and occasions of the political fact. The fitful
opaqueness in McKeon's own pedagogic discourse and writings is
paradoxically revealing. It tells of his involvement with the intractable multiplicities, contradictions, and approximations of the actual political-bureaucratic process. There was, as he taught by
example, so much more to the *vita activa* of the intellect than the
academy.

This truth was almost uncomfortably evident to Allen Tate. His
physique has remained legend. The vaulting forehead with its
beating artery; the hooded eyes in the manner, perhaps cultivated,
of Poe. The *ante-bellum* accent and delivery, at once exquisitely
courteous, indeed courtly, and charged with a flick of venom, of
feigned dismay, of condescension, were memorable. The very
name, "Tate," declared the compact finality of the bearer. His
presence at Chicago was emblematic of the novel alliance between
poet and professor, between novelist and seminar, representative
of the New Criticism and of the institution, first in the United

States, of collegiate courses in "creative writing." The consequences have, I believe, been damaging to literature and to most of
the true writers engaged in this Byzantine hybrid. But that is
another matter.

With just the right hint of saddened *hauteur,* Allen Tate let his
students know that he was among them by virtue of economic
necessity. That a *civitas* better-ordered, more in tune with the
sacerdotal functions of the poet – Augustan Rome, the Virginia or
Carolinas of the great plantations – would know how to look
properly after the needs of the author of the "Ode to the Confed-
erate Dead." Nonetheless, or because of his patrician code of duty,
Tate was a fine teacher. To a rare degree, his work had unified the
poetic with the critical process. Such poems as "Mr. Pope" and
Tate's version of the *Pervigilium veneris* are also illuminating acts of
critical interpretation and evaluation. Their tight form is one of
dramatized argument. In turn, Tate's best essays have a lyric finish.
The first assignment he gave us was to submit a pastiche of some
paragraphs in *The Dubliners.* The lesson intended was important.
Imitation comports understanding in depth. It does not hinge on
formal aping, on the variant reproduction of the vocabulary or
tricks of manner in the original. It succeeds (rarely) by recapturing
the underlying cadence, the tuning of expression to experience.
Having dismissed our clever little labors, Tate proceeded to read to
us, but so evidently to himself, a passage out of "The Dead." We
sat spellbound. Then that muted yet incisive voice: "Mr. Joyce,
you will note . . ."

A gothic imbroglio momentarily brought us close. The Bollin-
gen Prize for poetry had just been awarded to Ezra Pound's *Pisan
Cantos* (and not only "just" but justly). The jury included T. S.
Eliot and Allen Tate. A storm of protest broke. The judges were
accused of proto-fascist bias and of anti-Semitism. Among the

fiercest objectors was the poet and publicist Karl Shapiro. He fixed
on Tate's role as an unreconstructed southern agrarian, a notorious
anti-democrat, and a condemner of Jews. To have chosen Pound at
that moment in modern history was to have sacrificed critical
integrity to corrupt political ends.

I was asleep in the dormitory when a bemused night-watchman
came to inform me that Professor Tate (the Tates lived off campus)
would "value" – I recall the word – my immediate visit. I felt
panic. Was the summons a hoax? Had Tate read my latest seminar-
essay and taken it to be plagiarism? I trotted through the night in
mounting alarm. Allen Tate received me in immaculate shirt-
sleeves, a dramatically lowered lamp, and a bottle of Bourbon at
his gaunt elbow. The skull, as of ivory, shone. He apologized
ornately for the untimely summons. But the matter, I would surely
concur, could brook no delay. Was he justified – Tate lingered over
the participle – in assuming that I was Jewish? I mumbled assent.
Would I, in consequence, enlighten him as to whether or not a Jew
was, in the context of his faith and morals, at liberty to accept a
challenge to a duel? Mr. Tate was about to mail a cartel to Mr.
Shapiro in New York – he pointed to the pristine envelope. He
would not, of course, do so if Mr. Shapiro's Judaism made impossible a gentleman's positive response. All this in tones of cere-
moniously rounded good sense and serenity. My alarm must have
been palpable. I professed my inadequacy in so grave and delicate
a conundrum. Would Mr. Tate allow me to seek out those better-
versed in rabbinic law and practice? Oh indeed, he would. Might
he, in turn, count on word from me by the following evening?

It was not difficult, at the University of Chicago, to find *halachic*
authority. I was empowered to inform Professor Tate that Jewish
law granted freedom to the individual on points of honor. The days
that ensued were, for me, somewhat hallucinatory. Karl Shapiro

received the challenge, found it ludicrous, and published his exchange with Tate. This, in Tate's view – it may be in mine as well – put him beyond the pale. The episode flickered out like cold ash.

When, some years thereafter, I happened to recount it to Humphry House in his study at Wadham College, Oxford, House was unamused. Merriment, particularly with his students, was not House's strong suit. He had taken orders, and the ecclesiastical clung to him in lay life. He held himself in some kind of volcanic self-discipline, in the resolve not to allow too frequent rein to the anger, to the distaste inside him. Anger at the sloppiness of mundane institutions, notably academic; distaste at the vulgarity of the age. The strengths of technical editorial skills which underlie his labors on Gerard Manley Hopkins or on Dickens, the wisdom in his brief studies of Aristotle's poetics and of Coleridge (those superb, now neglected Clark Lectures), were, finally, of a religious-moralistic tenor. One simply had to get things right. Anything less was, in a very immediate sense, culpable, a sin against obligations of excellence which made endurable the fallen state of man. Incensed at the amateurism, at the complaisance of graduate studies in English at Oxford, House volunteered to run a research seminar. One day, he proceeded to detail Hopkins's school-boy cricket scores. Dutifully, heads down, we took notes. This time, Humphry House's rage made the casement windows quiver. "You idiots, incapable of even listening to what I'm saying and identifying it as garbage!"

Shortly before my doctoral *viva*, I called on House. On his Victorian lectern lay the handsomely printed text of my Chancellor's English Essay Prize. I waited, I ached for some allusion to it. It came when I was already at the door. "Ah yes, yes, your pamphlet. A touch dazzling, wouldn't you say?" The epithet fell like mid-winter.

After the refusal of my thesis, a first version of *The Death of Tragedy* (1961), I found absorbing, utterly educative work on the staff of the *Economist* in London. One afternoon, an awed commissionnaire announced to me the visit of a gentleman in a long black overcoat and wide-brimmed black hat. It was House. He asked if it was true that my thesis had received no proper supervision. It was. Did I wish to be taught seriously, thus making up for my own derelictions and what House knew to be the ways of too many of his colleagues? What little I know of textual scholarship, of bibliographic competence, of the use of primary sources and recensions, I owe to the hours House accorded me in Jermyn Street in London and at his private residence in Cambridge. I do not imagine that my dissertation on the failure of the English romantics to write successful plays, despite obsessive attempts, brought him much pleasure; or that he cared much for the central hypothesis (i.e., the "anti-tragic" thrust of English romanticism after the French Revolution). House felt he had to amend a flagrant injustice, a frivolity on the part of those who had left me untutored. Humphry House died suddenly and prematurely only days before my congratulatory re-examination. I can only hope that he had been apprised of the board's decision. Which was due wholly to the somber integrity of a just man.

There was anger as well in R. P. Blackmur, but its sources were ambiguous. Irascibility seeped from his sense of inadequate esteem, of marginalization even at Princeton and at the height of his renown. The world had not, he felt, priced his rare gifts at their true worth. A disheveled domestic past imposed on Blackmur recurrent financial straits. By the time I knew him, the nerve of poetry had more or less atrophied. Blackmur was preoccupied by T. S. Eliot's, and to a lesser extent by Allen Tate's twofold success in producing both poetry and sovereign criticism. He observed too closely the place in American literature of his fellow critic and teacher, John Crowe Ransom. Or of Robert Penn Warren, poet, novelist, critic. On bad days, Blackmur conjectured that his own performance might turn out to have been distinctive but minor, a somewhat secret flowering among *cognoscenti* or, as he preferred to call them, "amateurs," practitioners of arduous love.

My wife and I, new to marriage, saw much of Blackmur in our Princeton years. He invited me to give the prestigious Gauss Seminars. We met on European holidays. But the unforced trust, the heart's ease I aspired to stayed out of reach. Liquor ruled increasingly in a way of life at once gregarious and lonely. Those unwilling to consume seriously, to spin out the nights with Bourbon, to abide Blackmur's sodden moods, came to bore and even irritate him. A second inhibition was that of Blackmur's pleasure in playing off against each other, in manipulating competitively those who hoped too obviously for his critical endorsement, for the literary support and favors in his giving. It was an archly flirtatious game: to intimate to A that he was less talented, less deserving of notice than B; but to let B drop just when the academic testimonial, the nomination to a bursary, the mention in a review seemed assured. Like other human beings disillusioned, homeless in themselves, Blackmur read with feline precision the hopes, the needs in others. He drank deep of their disappointments.

Yet what a critic-commentator he was, and how acutely he analyzed the dilemmas of culture in American democracy. He brought to the elusive turbulence of creative acts, when these are under pressure of moral intuitions and of the imaginary, a rare exactitude of apprehension (his poetics owed much to Maritain). On T. S. Eliot, on Montaigne, on Thomas Mann's *Doctor Faustus,* on Henry Adams, his true begetter, Blackmur could be magisterial. He had read Dante with Maritain. His meditations on

Henry James, a process so sustained and empathic that it made of Blackmur's prose a pastiche of the master's, remain classics of encounter. In their turn, Blackmur's voice, the devices in his stylistic alchemy, cast a spell on younger practitioners. Here was a commitment to the primacy of literature, to the anarchic logic of the poetic which, when in complex flow, recalled the immediacies of Coleridge and Walter Benjamin's uncompromising adherence to the pulse of language within history.

For a time, I was mesmerized (though French *méduse*, with its element of petrification, might be more accurate). But we drifted apart. Blackmur's is an influence at once stimulating and important to relinquish. Today much of the work has faded altogether. It surfaces only occasionally among the voices which shape poetry and criticism. There is injustice in this eclipse and the tawdry verdict of fashion. Blackmur is too demanding, too compactly allusive for a literacy of fast foods. But his recession also contains a warning. Art and literature turn on those who would make of criticism, of commentary a rival and competing mode. Let down by his poetry, Blackmur burnished his prose to a pitch of obtrusive brilliance, of ornamentation so visible, so "palpably designed" (Keats's admonition) as to interpose itself between insight and object. To cite again the current shibboleth: text is made pre-text. Time deals harshly with this inversion.

Could there be a more trenchant contrast than that with Gershom Scholem? I shared guest-quarters with him in the Bodmer House at the University of Zurich. We met in Berne at the very café-table which he had frequented with Walter Benjamin during the close of the First World War. Scholem allowed me a number of visits to his book-devoured – how else can one put it? – home in Jerusalem. We corresponded.

Scholem had started out as a mathematician. This is, I believe, the key. Mathematics instills a zest for certainty, for conclusive demonstration. It was from his contact with higher mathematics that Gershom Scholem derived his conviction that extreme technical-formal difficulty, the maneuvers of analysis requiring taxing preparation, would, at the last, yield utmost clarity. There is for the mathematician no contradiction between what is impenetrable to common understanding and the revelation, to the initiated, of perfectly luminous and fundamental truths. Scholem's exposition of Jewish mysticism and Kabbalah is, in a sense, algebraic. The obscurity, the seeming esotericism of the material, like that, say, of elliptical functions, will, to those qualified by technical skill and unwavering concentration, uncover relations, mental spaces, and beauties of the rarest order. In no other intellect I have been privileged to meet, was there so decisive a refutation of Pascal's famous partition: in Scholem, the *esprit de finesse* was concomitantly that of *géométrie*. To him, as to the Neo-Platonists, the divine principle was, in its highest, arcane emanations, an analogue to pure mathematics.

Hence the provoking, sometimes bewildering rationality and dryness of Scholem's manner and approach. That Voltairean mien, the needling eyes, the bat's ears ever alert, the lips given to twists of sardonic dismay, composed a mask of reason. It pleased Scholem to exhibit texts, mental attitudes, beliefs of the most irrational, convoluted, even puerile provenance with tranquil good sense. Calmly, he took at face value fanaticism, esoterica, the jargon of the crazed heretic or mountebank. Scholem's analytic powers were entranced, though never suborned by, the fertility of unreason in the human psyche and in history. How that watchful, intensely private look sprang to impish life when Scholem chanced upon or chose to expound some choice fragment, some dimly glowing filament out of the mosaic of hermetic cosmogony, alchemy, or theosophy. His Zurich study, dark with late afternoon, sang with vitality (the hum of the sea in Prospero's cave) as he showed me a first photocopy of a tract, newly unearthed in Salonika, proving, as he had boldly conjectured, that a lineage of Sabbatarian heresy had survived covertly almost into modern times.

In Benjamin, Gershom Scholem had experienced an intuitive clairvoyance into the fabric of language and symbolism, a reasoned though metaphoric revelation as to the meanings of history, which he judged superior even to his own. Benjamin's labyrinthine refusal to emigrate to Palestine when there was still time, and the desolate death which followed, had left Scholem permanently bereaved – and exasperated. But he had found in Peter Szondi, the Swiss-German literary critic and literary historian, a stimulating younger colleague, a "shadow-Benjamin," as it were. Szondi's suicide, imitative of or possibly guided by that of Paul Celan, was yet a further, almost parodistic blow. Scholem would not gamble on intimacy again. Moreover, lacking Hebrew and being, in his considered estimate, a lesser presence than Szondi's, I could not engage Scholem's sustained interest. He allowed me to be a listener. He drew on what I could report to him of Anglo-American Judaism and of the saturnalia of post-structural and deconstructionist literary theories. Their pretentious nihilism confirmed his sardonic views. He was willing to consider my suggestion that these diverse movements stemmed from a characteristically Judaic rebellion against the paternalistic, logocentric burden of textuality, of Mosaic-Talmudic prescription. "That *is* possible; the rout of Korah. . . ," murmured Scholem, joining tight his long, expressive fingers.

He gave assent to my writing a review-profile at the time of the publication in English of the *magnum* on Sabbatai Zevi. He helped with certain biographical and contextual details. Scholem told memorably of his early struggles to get a hearing, let alone academic respectability for his study of Jewish mysticism and messianic expectations, these being so recurrently antinomian and heretical. Scholem had virtually created the field of which he was now master. (He allowed that I had faced a comparable situation when writing *After Babel.*) Yet all this evaded the crux. What did Gershom Scholem actually *believe?* Was he a religious man, a believer in God? What did he really make of the doctrines in the Kabbalah, in the Zohar, in the countless mystical-esoteric fantastications he had so incisively resuscitated? To put it crassly: what place in this analyst's and algebraist's soul had the forty-nine heavens and the angelic or demonic effusions which they lodged? I could not elicit any reply. The very question was chilled into impertinence. Thus I am left with the remembrance of an ironic agnostic, to whom all but a handful of other human beings were a disappointment, and who had found God, when he tested the concept, enigmatically ineffective. It was, precisely, this inefficacy and its tragic consequences for the history of the Jewish people which authorized, which in some ways necessitated, the kabbalistic-mystical incursion into emptiness.

Scholem may have met Donald MacKinnon at a colloquium in Rome. I am not sure. Scholem would, in any case, have found Donald's person perplexing. It is unusual for a professor of philosophic theology, known principally to his peers and students, to become in his lifetime the object of anecdotal legends so graphic that they helped inspire the figure of the metaphysician in Tom Stoppard's *Jumpers*. As a research Fellow at Balliol, MacKinnon had slipped under the high table and bitten in the shins an unendurable bore seated across from him. While lecturing in Cambridge, he had, in some rite of ultimate concentration (or reference to Occam's logic), ground a razor-blade into his palm.

During Fellows' meetings at his college, Corpus Christi, Professor MacKinnon had either bent over his own manuscript or book or had chewed through pencils, darkly unaware of the mesmerized silence around him. Seeing a colleague on the other side of the street, Donald had cordially bid him come to a dinner-party that evening. "But Donald, the party is in my honour!" D. M.: "Never mind, come anyway." The anecdotes, the myths mushroomed. None was as arresting as the man himself. Even in repose, the physique implied high drama. There was a prowling, leonine magnitude in Donald's stoop, in his myopic surge forward, in his searching hands. The voice was a manifold instrument, superbly played: it could, on the instant, ascend from a muffled, obscurely threatening growl to a pitch of merriment almost bird-like. The plangent snort which preceded MacKinnon's utterances was inimitable, though assiduously aped by his students and intimates.

At almost any time, Donald would fall – "plunge" is more precise – into a brown study, into fogged absences from those around him and the matter at hand. In part, these exits from immediacy arose from the dominance over him of memory. Donald MacKinnon's powers of recall were phenomenal in range and detail. He could summon to remembrance exam questions he had set forty years earlier, the maiden name of the aunt of a colleague encountered in the Highlands in boyhood. The exact pressure of recollection would cancel out the present. Entering Durham Cathedral, I confused "Ramsay" with "Ramsey," both names being prominent on marble plaques. Donald came to a monumental halt and delivered himself of a minute chronicle of these two episcopal-academic dynasties generations back. Like Coleridge on Hampstead Heath, MacKinnon would unravel his narrative whether or not the listener had slipped away.

In the course of teaching a revision class on Kant, Donald came
across a news item. The commanding officer of the French para-
chute regiments in Algeria had ordered his men to torture him,
with the identical means and obscenities inflicted on their Algerian prisoners. Having undergone this exercise, General Massu
announced that the pain was bearable, that the hideous reports
published about torture were weak-kneed exaggerations. "We will
now put Immanuel Kant aside," said Donald as he entered the
class. To him, this news-story embodied the fact of absolute, transcendent evil. It put in question not only Kant's providentialism
but the capacity of human reason to cope with extremities of
human conduct. To continue with an academic exegesis after reading such matter was inadmissible; or, rather, admissible solely if
an authentic relation could be shown between the monstrous in
Massu and Kant's ethics.

Blackness, a constant sense of the fragility of reason in the face
of irrationality and sadism, ached in MacKinnon. In a Pascalian
world, in which Jesus remained on the cross till the end of time,
reason was, to Donald, an intermittent gift of grace. It could, on
the hour, shiver into chaos and desolation. The roots of this over-
shadowing intimation of the tragic may well have been private. I
sometimes wondered whether some lasting shock attended on
Donald's "transportation" (the right word, I think) as a young boy
from life in Oban to a scholar's eminence and apartness at Win-
chester. Throughout the rest of his career, Donald and Lois, his
steadfastly perceptive wife, herself a distinguished painter, experienced England as exile. When breakdown seemed imminent, Lois
prevailed on Donald to leave Cambridge and return to Aberdeen.
But whatever the private elements, the work of the theologian and
philosopher was informed by a vision irrecusably somber. It was

this focus on suffering and injustice, sustained at obvious psychic risk, which set Donald MacKinnon apart, and which makes the finest of his writings and teaching tower over the surrounding flatlands of current Anglican divinity.

We saw each other very regularly in Cambridge and on all my home-visits from Geneva. Retired, Donald came to hear me lecture at Durham and in Glasgow (the 1990 Gifford Lectures). He was in King's Chapel, Cambridge, when I spoke in commemoration of the anniversary of the end of the two world wars. I owe to MacKinnon's essays, to his letters, to the years of dialogue, much of what is central to my later work. There could, for Donald, be no justifiable future for Christianity so long as Christian theology and practice had not faced up to, had not internalized lucidly, its seminal role in the millennial torments of Judaism and in the Holocaust. Primarily, this signified a coming to terms with the horror of Golgotha, a horror unredeemed – this was Donald's compulsive instinct – by the putative wonder of resurrection or by any promise of celestial reparation. Like Kierkegaard, whom he pondered assiduously, like Dostoevsky, MacKinnon was an imaginer, a questioner of Hell rather than of Heaven (the Scottish bias). When trying, haltingly, to find a symmetry of the inhuman between the Jewish refusal of the "man/god" Jesus and the deliberate bestialization of man, both as butcher and as victim, in the camps, when trying to "think" Auschwitz and Golgotha as implicated in some interrelated finality, I am carrying forward from the hours with Donald MacKinnon (cf. my book *No Passion Spent*, 1996).

One of the last times I saw him (I was thereafter sadly privileged to speak his *in memoriam* in Cambridge) was at a Corpus feast. Donald received me on the twilit lawn in full clan regalia, an archaic, sovereign figure against the evening glow. His welcome growled towards me. Since his death, the landscape is meaner.

MacKinnon's rages were legend. So have been those of Pierre Boutang. But whereas Donald labored under the pressure on his spirit of lasting death, Boutang celebrates, fiercely, a certitude of immortality in Christ. I left him, only recently, in his book-thronged eyrie in St. Germain, his sight failing, his skin and hands mottled with age, singing, in a cracked, exultant voice, almost a child's voice, an Easter hymn, a rhyme on resurrection. Boutang despises medicine with something of Molière's acerbity. He will not be seen to. That care is God's *métier*. Boutang rejoices at the prospect of "living his own proper death," of exploring that tran-sit, be it lacerating and humiliating, to ultimate unison with the Catholic church militant and triumphant. How abject it would be to muffle such adventure towards rebirth by the use of pain-killers or clinical artifice.

It may be that Pierre Boutang has never known fear. As a young *camelôt du roi,* a royalist and absolutist acolyte of Maurras and the *Action française,* Boutang, putting up inflammatory posters, was cornered by a dozen communists in a blind alley in Paris. He hurled himself at them and was left beaten almost to death. He has paid harshly for his allegiance, quixotic and violent, chivalric and scurrilous, to absurd ideals of monarchic restoration, of a the-ocracy in the style of de Maistre, Bossuet (and Solzhenitsyn). He has been a pamphleteer against Jews, whose mystery of survival obsesses him. On a mundane level, Pierre Boutang sees in the Jew the virus of secular, capitalist rationality after the "catastrophe" of the French Revolution. The Jews incarnate and exploit a damn-able modernity. On an eschatological level, in the unfathomable scenario of the *mysterium* of revelation, the Jews, by virtue of their rejection of the Messiah-Jesus, hold mankind to ransom. There can be, believes Boutang, no kingdom of love and of pardon on this earth so long as the Jew remains outside the *ecclesia.* At one of the portals of the Cathedral of Strasburg, Synagogue, blindfolded, and Church compassionate yet regal, confront each other across an abyss of unhoused hope. This abyss is our cruel history.

Boutang is intoxicated with poetry, with a knowledge, extensively by heart, of Dante, Scève, and Blake. His translation of Plato is poetry. He has written what I take to be one of the major philosophic texts in the century: *L'Ontologie du secret*. Scarcely known, this exceedingly difficult treatise is, like Hegel's *Phenomenology*, a voyage through spaces of thought, circling back on itself, demanding to be lived as well as read. It deals, to put it far too naïvely, with that which underlies, which empowers metaphor. What "absences" are implicit in predication? When we forget, where has the "forgotten" gone, from where does it return? If perception and metaphor are, as Plato has it, arcs of sudden relation, flung bridges, what lies "underneath" them? It may, as with Kierkegaard, take generations before *L'Ontologie* is understood, before it enters the mainstream of epistemological argument. But it will, I am confident, do so.

My closeness to Boutang – his political-activist past, his joyous intolerance have left him isolated – is an obvious improbability. But the debates we have had, both in public and private, are among the stellar hours in my life. We share an utter passion for Scripture and the classics, for poetry and metaphysics. We delight in the kind of teaching that is an act of shared love (I have watched Boutang initiate one of his numerous grandchildren in New Testament Greek). We both know that learning *by heart* is precisely that. Dialectically divided, he and I are at one in intuiting that the question of the existence, of the conceivability or negation of God, however one approaches it, reinsures seriousness of mind and spirit. That it is, at the last, the continuum, the meaning of meaning under the arching miracle of language, of art, of music and philosophy. How can this inspired man – Aquinas, Dante, and Pascal always at his elbow – have spoken, written, acted as he did during the 1930s and, his enemies allege, during the Second World War? I suspect that there may be a self-disdaining fascination with Boutang's physical *bravura* in my feelings towards him. I am, most likely, a coward, contemptibly incapable of unthinking courage. What made me insist on Pierre Boutang's presence at my lectures at the Collège de France, and shiver with anger when the officious mandarins and liberal pontiffs in the hall refused to shake the old man's hand? Only Montaigne has the answer: "Because he is he, because I am I."

Boutang and I were introduced by Alexis Philonenko. Philonenko's intellect is one of the most astringent in Europe. We dined weekly during our academic terms in Geneva. Depending on his humor, Alexis can be seductive, coruscating company. He plays the French language with studied virtuosity. At other occasions, he will immure his untiring train of thought, the current of abstraction which beats in him, in a monologue only partly audible, directed inward and wreathed in a chain-smoker's dun halo. The constancy of focus, the discard of waste motion, are awesome. Philonenko embodies the antithesis to free association. I have seen him riveted to one spot or weaving across a road unheeding when in the stringently sequential grip of analytic thought. Alexis's output is phenomenal: some twenty or more books, many of them voluminous. This prodigality is made possible by an undeflected concentration. He writes on trains and in buses, between classes or into the night. His prose can be as tight as his thought. In his best work, the commentaries on Kant and on Fichte, the essays on the philosophy of war and Tolstoy, the full-scale study of the young Feuerbach, the three-volume, acute inquiry into the theme of *malheur* in Rousseau, Philonenko nails his prose to the exact bone-structure of demonstration. There are no rhetorical flourishes, no lacunae for indeterminacy. Alexis looks longingly towards mathematics. Where it succeeds, his idiom is algebraic. Hence his expert admiration for Leibniz and for Bergson, mathematicians both.

Such matters are too serious for urbanity. I recall the evening walk in the Old City in Geneva when Alexis staked out the contours of our relationship. First came the veritable makers, the original thinkers, the begetters of systematic philosophy. He adduced Plato, Aristotle, Descartes, Kant, or his beloved Fichte. Second, there are the fully-qualified expositors and historians of philosophy (these two functions being, if rightly practiced, almost identical). These can deploy the labors of the masters at the requisite technical level and place them accurately within the aggregate of Western speculative discourse. Such analytic historians (e.g., Philonenko) are rare. In third rank, at some vaguely disqualifying remove, come the *literati,* the essayists, critics, intellectual historians, and the immense majority of pedagogues and academics so mordantly categorized by either Rabelais or Hegel. At best their chatter entertains, at worst it produces pretentious muddle. There could be scant room for doubt as to which of these three classes I belonged to. No odium attached to Alexis's dictate; simply a realism at once melancholy and amused. This was how providence, magisterial in its irrevocable labels, had ordained. (Like Aron, like Sartre, Philonenko had graduated first in the ferociously competitive *agrégation* examinations.) Why fret at one's own mediocrity? After which he exhaled a wisp of smoke into the night air. Much later, in a published work, Alexis opined that my lectures had exceptional merit, that they had held even him spell-bound. But such *brio,* he added, cast its shadow on the written work.

Nevertheless, we have grown close. Over two decades, our correspondence has been uninterrupted. There have been intimacies of reason and of feeling in the Philonenko apartment, with its matchless view of the Trocadéro and Eiffel Tower. Monique Philonenko is a bastion of skeptical strength. I am not, by temperament, the best of listeners. With Alexis, I try to be. If only to register the *finesse,* the unswerving logic always at work below the surface of speech. It is fascinating and instructive to be in range of a man or a woman who does not think part-time, whose corporeal modes of presence "body forth" thought. There has also been some similitude in our circumstance. Feared for his unsparing criteria regarding academic scholarship, for his acerbities, for his arrogant impatience, which is in fact a rage for excellence, Monsieur Philonenko has been marginalized. The Sorbonne, the Collège de France, replete with laureled mediocrities, would have none of him. His chairs have been at Caen, Geneva, and Rouen. Many of his books have been passed under virtual silence. The circus folk of deconstruction and poststructuralism bear him particular ill will. Alexis holds them in derision, points to their logical confusions, and regards his lamed career as a necessary tribute to seriousness. Moreover, has he not written a history of boxing which became a best-seller and for which the French ministry of sport bestowed on him a national citation? We differ on boxing, and on teaching. An almost autistic historian of the mind, Philonenko long aspired to retirement. Teaching had been an often fruitless chore. It is, to me, indispensable. Even my fiction derives from it. Which merely confirms Alexis's verdict. *Mais on s'aime bien.*

It is my love of teaching which would make incomplete a chapter on those who have taught me if it did not mention a handful of my own students in the United States, Cambridge, and Geneva. The signal reward for a teacher is to engage students whom he discovers to be abler than himself, whose capabilities will, ought to, generate achievements beyond his own. Even in the proudest institutions of learning, such engagement is infrequent. It has been granted to me at least four times. When, at a first meeting in my Geneva office, I pointed out to B. S. that doctorates in comparative literature entailed few prospects of gainful employment, he shot back: "There is always your chair, Monsieur." And proceeded to exhibit linguistic-stylistic talents in excess of my own (almost predictably, he turned on me thereafter). Trapped in bitter shyness, E. D. would not, for some weeks, even discard her overcoat during our Cambridge supervisions. After dazzling finals, she came to let me know of her abhorrence of the academic humanistic outlook, of her commitment to Maoism and medical service among the destitute of western China. S. G. has flowered into public prominence in English studies in the United States. He has founded a movement in literary theory. He is a superb academic politician, using his strategic tact and energies to good purpose. Something deeper, more guarded ought to have come of his acclaimed writings. He knows that I feel this, and also intend it as a compliment to one so formidably endowed. I sensed in M. S. a sort of heat-lightning, fitful but of a brilliance such as to transform the horizon. Here was a scholar-exegete of radical originality, putting himself and his work under extreme cerebral-emotional stress. M. could make things new. Though it draws, often transparently, on my own work, M.'s writing leaves this fact strictly unmentioned. Far more fashionable, useful patrons lie to hand. University stardom and the rubric "genius" have resulted. The books produced have not altogether borne out the promise. Recent examples are close to being out of control, spiraling almost tragically into arcane self-regard.

Be that as it may, these four students, one Genevese, one Welsh, and two American-Jewish (as well, no doubt, as others) have been among my teachers. Thanks be.

10

Genius loci, the "spirit of place," which, like an unbidden bolt of recognition, transforms a landscape, a street-corner into "inscape," into a reorientation of awareness. Snow was blowing and drifting in a white fog. The rural road simply vanished. My wife, whose sagacity of heart, radiant good sense, and unspoken perceptions are incomparable, drove parallel with what we could make out of fence-posts. At moments even these blanked out in a white tumult. Suddenly, the February blizzard cleared. A cold brilliance washed the air. We edged the car across the fields back to a paved road and into woods. A gently tortuous descent led from the plateau. On either side, like scarred walls, towered the cliffs painted time and again by Courbet in this corner of the Franche-Comté. A breach opened in the larch, pale birch and black pine. Zara and I stopped breathless. Below us, in the perfectly rounded cusp of the hills, traversed by a stream whose crystal voices reached us even far above, lay a hamlet. Its rust-colored and snow-blown roofs, squat church-tower and two small chateaux – the one ramshackled and Second Empire, the other a pure marvel of a seventeenth-eighteenth century *logis* and circular *donjon* – composed a compact, earth-bound yet also mirage-like ensemble. We were struck mute with wonder. The church clock rang its hour as we crossed the low stone bridge, its querulous chime somehow answered by the toss of silver-white and green-ochre (Courbet's palette) of water across lustrous stones. I knew at once that there would be for me no greater perfection anywhere, that I had stumbled on home. This certainty has been confirmed each time I have returned.

The diverseness of the hills as they couch around the village is difficult to define. The plateau breaks off on one flank into a wooded escarpment, gouged by erosion and fallen limestone. Half buried among stricken logs and boulders on the crest immediately above N. are the remains of a Gallic camp and trench-work. Westward, a single-lane road followed by a dirt track and, finally, a sodden footpath leads into a vale of myriad shadows and secretive gusts. An isolated farmstead, its barn implausibly large, marks the ascent to a small col. The *hameau* itself abuts on a monumental cliff, whose base is hollowed into a soaring arch where the river has its source. Near the rim of the great cliff are the erratic vestiges, somewhat arduous to reach and make out, of the small military keep to whose ephemeral role in the wars and politics of Charles V of Spain and Flanders, N. owes its sole footnote in history. To the east, past heights infolded like stone drapes, through bluebell woods and meadows, the walk climbs to a curved summit. On clear days, this belvedere allows a view of much of the Franche-Comté and, on the veiled horizon, of the Jura. Sparrow-hawk wheel almost incessantly above the rocks; in season, the stream is alive with speckled trout; one end-of-winter night, I heard the flinty drumming of hooves as boars passed on their annual migration.

But even these natural wonders are not the essence. I have, throughout my too loquacious life, been a collector of silences. These are getting harder and harder to find. Noise – industrial, technological, electronic, amplified to the pitch of madness (the "rave") – is the bubonic plague of capitalist populism. Not only in the media-sodden West, but among the tin shacks of African shanty-towns or the multitudes of Shanghai. Only the privileged or the deafened manage to hear themselves be. The silences in that lost corner of the Franche-Comté are, obviously, and praise God, outside any language. They are manifold. The nights are, in some manner, made even more silent by the muted tumble of the stream and the haunting snap of branches in the forests. There is a silence as of a far-off white fire at sunrise, when the ancient chill of rock and stone walls drains out of the receding shadows. Noon has a silence all its own, torn on occasion by a belated, knife-edged clarion of roosters. The silences in N. are indescribably alive. They inhabit the altering light as it moves, under the play of clouds, across the hollow. Paradoxically, there is a silence at the heart of the great winds, of the lash and turbulence of the wind-storms which guard this haven from the tourist. In the not infrequent mists which carry with them the scent of pine-needles and wet granite, one hears like a silence of silence.

There have been in my existence far too many bellowing cities, airports, and far, far too much talk (*mea culpa maxima*). As my hearing wanes, the pounding of rock music in the Manhattan taxi, the chatter of cellular phones, seem to worsen. Wherever I find myself in bedlam or, more exactly, have lost myself, I focus my mind and imagination on N. I summon to memory, to expectation, that human scale, that dark harvest of historical time and of timelessness. I bring to recollection the small marble plaque in the church vestibule on which are the names of the fallen of 1914–18, 1939–45, and the Algerian war (two families have lost three each). Above all, I reach out for that bounty of silences. For better or for worse – silence is also a strict examiner – I am, in that talismanic spot, housed in myself, a freeholder at last.

Silence is not the forte of West 47th Street, between Fifth and Sixth Avenues in mid-town New York City. The street hums and quivers perpetually like a high-voltage cable. It is lined on both sides by jewelers and emporia for the purchase and sale of gold, silver, and precious stones. A cornucopia of trash-treasures, engagement- and wedding-bands by the gross fill the shop windows. Serious offerings and transactions, silk-paper rustling in the palm, are played out in the back rooms. But the carnival proceeds on the pavements. Jewish dealers, brokers, stone-cutters, middle-men, and kibbitzers throng the sidewalk. Their garb spans the entire gamut of Orthodox and Conservative styles, from sober mufti and discrete skull-caps all the way to the long black gabardine, broad-brimmed black hats or fur bonnets, and *tephilim* (the ritually inscribed, talismanic phylacteries) of the Hasidim. Some men are clean-shaven, a goodly number moderately bearded, and the Hassidic brethren rejoice in prophetic beards and side-locks. The tribes on 47th Street are out of Babel. The beehive thrum of voices which hangs in the air is compounded of Hebrew, Yiddish, Polish, Russian, Ukrainian, and peppery draughts of Manhattan-Brooklyn-Bronx American. The chorus swells to a climax at certain hours of the day, notably before prayers. The street boasts its own synagogue, behind doors identical to those of business. The pulse of speech, from stentorian whispers to imperious calls, throbs continuously. Offers are made and haggled over; bargains struck; favors, credit, and gossip traded. A barbed rhetoric sprung from Talmudic debate and quibbling, the gambit of the *raconteur* (sarcasm has its lyrics), of the peddler of proverbs, the feline pathos cultivated in the constriction of the east-European ghetto and *Stättle,* draw traders into sudden knots, blocking the pavement and, no less brusquely, unraveling.

Patriarchs hover in known doorways, harvesting the young who, when they are of rigidly Orthodox observance, exhibit the thinned faces and tired eyes of the student in rabbinic schools.

Hands glide in and out of cavernous pockets, and for a mere instant the light catches the flicker of gold or of a diamond. Shoulders shrug in feigned indifference or underestimate, comprising nuances of denial, of stifled hopes, of tactical arrogance as traditional, as sorrowful as is the Diaspora itself. It is this body language which mesmerizes. It is the day-long dance of the men in black – no women, of course – as they weave back and forth in dialogue, in prolix display, in razor-honed commerce. Up and down the block, from the south corner to the north, mazing intricate patterns of avoidance and collision, of recognition and rivalry. For the Hasid the line between secular, mercantile discourse and the monologue for God in formulaic prayer is hair-thin. Lips move without pause. The body, now in exile in Manhattan, sways forward towards the Sacred Wall in Jerusalem in front of which it will, assuredly, strike its final bargain and dance its last dance. For is this diamond, be it a fraction of a carat, not that of Solomon?

Nestling between the jewelers is New York's most literary bookstore, and one of the last in any serious sense. In the 1940s there was a veritable pride of second-hand book-stores south of 14th Street and down Broadway. These were, on Saturdays, my other school. One could browse voraciously. Having, impudently, commended to a hesitant buyer the costly, plum-clad New York edition of Henry James, I was rewarded by the amused book-seller with the Bohn Library Vasari which I had transparently coveted during preceding months and which I treasure still. Today, the Gotham Book Mart on 47th Street is among the last of the Mohicans. Its walls are papered with photographs, usually signed, of Joyce, T. S. Eliot, Frost, Auden, Faulkner, and more recent powers. It stocks back-numbers and runs of "little magazines," once indispensable to the life of literature and the mind, today struggling for ephemeral hearing. The Gotham seeks to display the poetry put out by small presses and isolated imprints. Illustrious poets, playwrights, and novelists have read and autographed in that crowded basement. As they assume airs of familiarity, clients hope to be mistaken for true *literati* (of late, those who run the Gotham have become, almost regrettably, less acerbic). When I visit, which is to say on every return to New York City, I am shown a little list of misguided collectors looking out for this or that of my very early publications – the verse, the Oxford prize essay, the first issue of *Language and Silence.* The caress is irresistible: I leave the Gotham with purchases I never intended.

The traders in jewels and precious metals and that bookmart; the Hasidim and the works and portraits of some of the minstrels of anti-Semitism – Pound, Eliot, Céline. The cheap rings that bind love and the costly poetry which celebrates or mourns it. The continguity on West 47th is inexhaustible.

When it angles across light, rain can enhance. On reddish-gray romanesque walls it spins a web whose knots and filaments are silver. It would, in any event, be difficult to imagine weather in which Girona, in Catalonia, could not cast its spell. The riches are prodigal: the convents of *la Mercé,* of Sant Domènec, of Sant Francesc, the church of Sant Feliu; the chapels of St. James and of Saint Michael; above all, the *Seu,* the massive fortress-basilica unto God. Which houses the sepulchre of the Countess Ermessenda, *anno* 1385. This is one of the little-known but absolute summits of Gothic art, of all art pure and simple. Hewn in alabaster, the visage is that of sleep itself, of a welcomed solemnity of repose behind whose closed lids and breathing mouth the sculptor hints at an incipient smile. But "smile" may be the wrong word. It is from within the carved stone that there glows a secret of light, of reticent valediction. The economy of line, the antinomy of sensuous, even sensual, abstraction, will not be matched again until Brancusi. If absolute beauty is already the guest of death, Guillem Morell's figure is the proof.

I had hived off from our party. I found myself in the huddled lanes and masked inner courtyards of the medieval Jewish quarter, unnervingly but also logically close to the cathedral precinct (medieval ecclesiastics offered fitful, extortionary safeguard to "their" Jews). Thick shadow and rainfall washed across the low archways and cobble-stones. A street-sign marked the narrow passage as that of the renowned Kabbalist, Isaac the Blind. Somewhere hereabouts the sightless seer had practiced his occult mysteries. A handful of disciples – Kabbalists are allowed only two or three adepts for instruction – had come to this silent warren. They must have heard, as I now did, the vesper bells of the *Seu* in the midst of their arcane arts.

Staring at the worn flight of steps which led into a further recess, I saw the lineaments of a very old man, a fleck of ebbing light on his forked beard, returning my stare out of dead eyes. Fantasy and place had contrived a specter, a momentary condensation and in-gathering of time into shape. Then the shadow dissolved into thicker shadows and the gloom took with it the point of light. It is, I believe, this informing brush of time's hand, of the subconsciously felt pressures of history, more often than not tragic, on physical surroundings, on roof-lines and landscape, even, at enigmatic instants, on rivers and winds, which is most vivid to Europe. Without this palpable presence of human temporality, we could not have the fathomless geography – those vineyard-crowded hills, the girt villages, the inhabited skies, the panoramas of towers and steeples in the background of Renaissance Passions or beyond the casements of a Van Eyck. By contrast, so much of American space, hence its seductive liberality, is, as yet, extraterritorial to human thought and pain. It is timeless in its forgiving indifference. European time, that sand-paper, as it were, of unquenched history, is at work on that alabaster in Girona, on a Brancusi profile or the cry out of a Bacon, as they are not in regard to the free flight of a Calder, in its casual lift-off from mortality.

"American time" and American investments in the immediate, in the "happening" and its playful refusal of remembrance, are now in the ascendant. The relations between time and individual death, relations both social and metaphoric, biomedical and alle-goric, which have been the calendar of classic European thought, aesthetics, and social conventions, are altering. The proud patience, the wager on lastingness, on durance, which in different but kindred ways inspired the tomb of the Countess and the sometimes crazed acrobatics of numerological, alchemical, gram-matological speculation ("mirroring") in the chamber of Isaac the Blind, is no longer in force. In ways as yet incalculable, this seismic shift to the "present future," the defining North American and, probably, East Asian verb tense, will transmute not only our tech-nologies but also the arts and the habits of consciousness itself. A Picasso remains organically close to the master-builders and carv-ers of Girona. Duchamp and Tinguely, the *objet trouvé* and the "self-destruct," do not. Isaac the Blind would have pored with fascination over *Finnegans Wake*. Cyberspace is of a new world.

There have been too many hotels in my existence. But there are three on whose terraces or at whose windows I stand star-struck; for they front directly on three sovereign rivers.

Traffic on the Rhine is no longer what it was. Barges still pass, however, on the soft curve of the river as it traverses Basel. Their coughing chug draws closer and away. At night, their navigation lights glide past the balconies of the Trois Rois. On the facing bank, lies France and, just to one side, Germany. The Alsatian hills and vineyards trace the near horizon. Roman Catholic and Reformation Europe, French and German, meet along a river which, from its insignificant source in the glaciers all the way to the estuary of Rotterdam, has borne the ceremonies and hatreds, the musical-literary motifs and pollution of European history. Basel is Erasmus's city and Nietzsche's, keeping its embarrassed lights on so as to proclaim neutrality to the bomber-fleets streaming nightly into the French and German black-out at the close of the Second World War.

The Arno, by contrast, is mute and supine in its sand-tinted, almost marsh-like repose. In Florence, only the occasional skiff or flat-bottomed row-boat crosses an aged water. Yet exactly as in the chronicles of the medieval and Renaissance city, an intimation of abrupt waking, of menace is unmistakable. When the Arno floods, it seeps destructively into streets and squares. The reflections in the drowsing current are always unsteady, as if the Arno held the palaces and facades along its quays hostage. Till the next bout of sullen fury. Here too there is a hotel balcony facing towers and cupolas.

On clear mornings, the Limmat is as elegant, as patrician as its famous swans. It descends, in its busy, crystalline pace past the double towers of Zurich's minister towards the far peaks of the Berner Oberland. It is a river meditated on by Joyce and by Blackmur. As subtly urbane as the hotel Zum Storchen where Nelly Sachs met with Paul Celan, occasioning, in the shared after-death of the Holocaust, one of the indispensable poems in the German language. Clichés can serve as a shorthand for truths. Rivers *are* allegories of time. They set bridges in motion.

Even under the direst of communist East German bureaucracy, Weimar benefited from small mercies. Its prodigious cultural heritage kept certain officious brutalities at one remove. When I returned, after the collapse of the Berlin Wall and the DDR, vulgarization looked to be more blatant than freedom. The Elephant, the hostel beloved by Goethe, by Liszt, by Thomas Mann, is now a tarted-up pastiche of an American motor-inn. The antiquarian book-store where I once unearthed treasures is a stripped ghost of its former self. What remains intact (and unvisited) is a small cemetery on the way to the chateau. A number of gravestones lie fallen; the grass is rank. This is the burial-site of Russian infantry who died at the approaches to Weimar when the war was virtually over. No more, I reckon, than thirty or forty graves. A fair number are those of boy-soldiers, aged sixteen or seventeen, out of the Asian steppe, out of Kazakhstan and Turkmenia, done to death in a land and language of which they could have had no notion, by the insensate, robotic resistance and military skills of a moribund *Reich*. This unnoticed graveyard makes manifest the moronic waste and waste and waste of war, the appetite of war for children. Yet it expounds no less the mind-numbing affinities between war and high culture, between bestial violence and the noon places of human creativity. The bounds of Goethe's garden are minutes away to one side. The alleys familiar to Liszt and to Berlioz skirt the rusted gate. There is rest here, but no peace.

Marvels have been allowed me: the whip-lash line of changing colors off Cape Town, when the mauve of the Indian Ocean meets the green of the South Atlantic; the leviathan hump of Ithaka at first light; the incendiary set of sun, the dunes made molten copper, in the Negev; the undertow booming of the tides charging the cliff-portals of Etretat on the Norman coast; the sunken roads leading, apparently, into nowhere or into ghost-towns in Nevada; a storm boiling up out of that twenty-first-century bay in Hong Kong; the smoldering, pin-point embers in the eyes of jackals keeping their distance from the fire-pit in a visitors' lodge in

Kruger National Park; the scent of sulfur and of salt on the Icelandic tundra (is there any more entranced land?); the tap of thousands, of tens of thousands of footsteps hurrying to line the route of Winston Churchill's funeral procession in an otherwise totally silent, pre-dawn London; those volcanic cones literally floating, like gondolas hewn of snow, on the venomous smog which blankets Mexico City. But all this is tourism. In N., it will be tenure.

11

Errors grow more unbearable as they become irreparable.

I have scattered and, thus, wasted my strengths. The essays in *Language and Silence* called for a lifetime of concentrated development. "The Retreat from the Word," work on which dates back to the late 1950s, argues *in nuce* the incipient break of the contract between word and world, between semantic markers and stable sense which became the thesis of deconstruction and postmodernism. It foretold the "end of the great stories." In "Night Words," the debate of these past decades on pornography, on possible links between the sadism inherent in the pornographic and imitative human behavior, is set out. A number of essays introduced to English-speaking readers the Frankfurt School, the writings of Walter Benjamin, of Ernst Bloch, of Adorno, which have, since, become a critical-academic industry. "The Hollow Miracle" urged the conviction that totalitarian lies and savagery, notably in the Third *Reich* but also in other regimes, were conjoined to the corruption of language and, in turn, fueled by such corruption. This proposal has been widely taken up and detailed (it is itself, of course, indebted to Karl Kraus and to Orwell). So has the plea which underlies the entire book: that any serious consideration of the barbarism of our century, of the frustration of Enlightenment hopes and promises, must be closely knit to the "language-crisis" immediately preceding and following on 1914–18. This crisis is as germane to Wittgenstein's *Tractatus* as it is to the final, despairing cry to Schoenberg's *Moses und Aron;* it relates to the bacchanalia of *Finnegans Wake* and the tautologies of Gertrude Stein as closely as it does to Paul Celan's attempt at reinventing a language "north of the future."

Any one of these taxing themes necessitated consequent demonstration and deepening. Any one of them could have led to recognized mastery of a field in the history of ideas, in the philosophy of language and of culture, in poetics; to collaborative research in the academy, in institutions of advanced study which were to become both collective and specialized. The fundamental challenge I voiced – "How are we to grasp psychologically, socially, the capacity of human beings to perform, to respond to, say, Bach or Schubert in the evening, and to torture other human beings the next morning? Are there intimate congruities between the humanities and the inhuman?" – was taken up by others, more often than not without reference to its source. As was a question I put later: "Why the prodigality of homo-erotic contributions to the arts, to literature, to philosophy, and the near-total absence of any such role in the sciences?" (I am still waiting for an answer.)

But already, I had turned elsewhere. To the study of classical myths and their possible roots in the genesis of grammar (*Antigones,* 1984). To the mapping of philosophy and hermeneutics in *After Babel,* a work which, as I have mentioned, was pillaged and quarried both by those who passed it under silence and by the very journals and academic centers for "translation studies" which it helped initiate. The short book on Heidegger (1978) is now available in ten languages. And there has been the fiction. Such was the response to *The Portage to San Cristobal of A. H.* (1976), and to Alec McCowan's overwhelming interpretation on stage of the dominant figure, that I could have made of the novel or novella my foremost business. Yet again I tacked and altered course, returning to literature and philosophy, with something of a "theological" bias, in *Real Presences* and *No Passion Spent*.

The consequences have been difficult. Today, the "polymath" – the English use of the term conveys a particular sneer – is distrusted. He has few colleagues. He will commit errors and oversights, perhaps trivial or readily corrected, but of a kind which exasperates the specialist, which casts doubt on the work as a whole. I have, on occasion, been careless over detail, over technical discriminations. Impatience, a disinclination to submit work in progress to expert scrutiny, the pressure of deadlines and public platforms – too numerous, too diverse – have marred texts which could have been, formally at least, unblemished. An unripe restlessness, *bougeotte* in French, has made me drop subjects, problems, disciplines once I thought, erroneously perhaps, that I had seized their gist, that I knew where the matter led. My belief that cows have fields but that passions in motion are the privilege of the human mind has long been held against me.

Conceivably, it is no longer legitimate for any one individual to publish on ancient Greek literature and on chess, on philosophy and the Russian novel, on linguistics and aesthetics; perhaps it is no longer advisable to hold university chairs while writing fiction and contributing more than 150 review-essays to the *New Yorker*, where, in late 1966, I was asked to help fill the gap left by Edmund Wilson. Even where something of genius is in play, as in a Koestler, the risks are steep. To smaller gifts, they may be damning. As the close comes nearer, I know that my crowded solitude, that the absence of any school or movement originating in my work, and that the sum of its imperfections are, in considerable measure, of my own doing. The appropriation, the exploitation of my writings and teaching by others, the blatant non-acknowledgment by those who have found its public visibility and variousness offensive may, by ironic paradox, be its true reward. But the sadness, the *tristitia,* that numbing Latin word, is there.

Moreover, despite antennae exceedingly alert to the changing "spirit of the age," I apprehended too late certain key shifts. Aware, early on, of the widening authority of the mathematical and experimental sciences, intensely involved in the "language-revolution" and the coming of the new media of meaning, I nonetheless did not identify rigorously the underlying tectonic drift. Educated in a hypertrophied reverence for the classics, in that near-worship of the "titans" of thought, music, literature, and the arts, so characteristic of emancipated Central European Judaism, I felt committed to the canonic, the confirmed, and the "immortal" (those *immortels* mummified in the French Academy!). It took too long before I understood that the ephemeral, the fragmentary, the derisive, the self-ironizing are the key modes of modernity; before I realized that the interactions between high and popular culture, notably via the film and television – now the commanding instruments of general sensibility and, it may be, of invention – had largely replaced the monumental pantheon. Influential as they are, deconstruction and postmodernism are themselves only symptoms, bright bubbles at the surface of a much deeper mutation. It is, as I have suggested, our elemental perceptions of death, our time-sense, of the related classical impulse in art and poetry to endure, to achieve timelessness which are, today, in radical question. It is the transformation of these ontological-historical categories, in Kant's sense of the word, it is the ebbing of ideals and performative hierarchies instrumental since the pre-Socratics, which define what I have called "the epilogue" but which others acclaim as "the new age." There is too much I have grasped too late in the day. Too often my activity as a writer and teacher, as a critic and scholar, has been, consciously or not, an *in memoriam*, a curatorship of remembrance. But could it be otherwise after the Shoah?

Psychoanalysis fills me with incredulity. It is, at its brief best in Freud, a mythological narrative of genius. The notion of my father as a sexual rival, of some universal "Oedipal complex" (long refuted by anthropology) seems to me irresponsible melodrama. My father was, and remains long after his death in 1968, the indispensable friend, the exigent partner in dialogue. Nevertheless, there may be a mustard-seed of truth in the psychoanalytic conjecture that an overthrow, a physically homicidal erasure of one's father-figure is necessary to independence; that there can be, without such rebellion, neither sufficient originality nor will to power. It may be that too much of my father's "library," of his "syllabus" of the supreme and caustic certitude that in the face of a Homer, of a Goethe, of a Beethoven or a Rembrandt, the second-rate is precisely that, conditions and confines me still. As did his skepticism in regard to direct political action.

On one issue, at least, and which now seems to me vital, such abstention may prove unforgivable. I have already referred to my sense of Israel as an *indispensable miracle,* but one tragically marked by its contradictions to the ethical, universalist genius of unhoused Judaism. Persistently, I have asked whether the core-meaning of Judaism can be reconciled with the realities of an armed nation-state surrounded by pitiless and cynical enemies. As I have said, Israel, like all other nations, has to torture to survive. But is even survival a justification? Can Judaism and the moral aim of its calling recover? What I now know is this: only those prepared to live in Israel, under the immediacies of danger and in the places of hatred, have the full right to pose this question, to address their anguish to it. It has been too easy, possibly too self-flattering, to be the "idiot-questioner" (Blake) from outside. Here, as well, I have flinched.

Regrets: that I did not carry on drawing, in charcoal, chalks, and India inks so as to illustrate some of my own books. The hand speaks truths and joys which the tongue cannot. That I did not learn Hebrew, which alone allows direct access to the Bible and to the inward of Jewish identity, when my friend and assistant in Geneva, Ami Dykman, was more than ready to teach me. *Accidia*, sloth of spirit (is it now too late?). I regret not having taken up the offer of a Cambridge colleague, a pathologist of proven insight and tact, to try LSD under his supervision. Having experienced no such drug, I remain at a loss to imagine, to conceptualize one of the principal agents of ruin and of consolation, of desire, and of annulment at the anarchic heart of our culture. A "trip" not taken. And why did I not, when starting salaried life in London during the early 1950s, borrow the money needed, a modest sum, to acquire a small Ben Nicholson, as in-gathered, as mysteriously lit as is any Chardin. Had I done so, its serene logic would be with me still. Was it my father's adherence to Polonius's "neither a lender nor a borrower be"?

On a recent drive through rural Ohio, I saw signs put up by a local real estate dealer. Instead of the customary "Sold," these read: "Sorry, too late." Exactly so. If there are tombstones for hope, this is their epitaph.

Speaking of the enigmatic, bitter history of Judaism, I have used the phrase "intimacy with God." What meaning can an adult, rational intellect, at the end of the millennium, attribute to such words? What sense other than fictive, metaphoric, or conventionally retrospective (historical) can they possibly communicate, let alone submit to serious analysis? The case for atheism is compelling. The stoic sanity, the lucid demand for evidence which it entails, deserve respect.

As it has always been, theodicy is the crux. If God is, why does He tolerate the glaring horrors and injustice of the human condition? He may be a malevolent potentate, torturing, humiliating, starving, killing men, women, and children as "wanton boys do flies." He may be a deity of circumscribed or exhausted powers. Though it has been the sub-text of my fiction, the concept of a lamed or powerless God verges on the absurd. Immemorially, attempts to "justify His ways to man" have drawn on the cruel paradox of freedom. Men and women must be allowed freedom of choice and of action, including that of doing evil to others and themselves. How else could there be merit and responsibility? There are fables of compensation: unjust suffering shall be rewarded in eternity. None of these three narratives – the diabolical, the impotent, the compensatory – commends itself to reason. Each, in its own manner, offends intelligence and morality. The answer given to the question posed during the torture and hanging of a starving child at Auschwitz ("Where now is God?," "God is that child") is a more or less nauseating bit of anthropomorphic pathos.

The argument from the Cross, the doctrine of sacrificial expiation and the scapegoat transferred from man – Abraham and Isaac – to the Christian God-father and His only begotten Son, can only convince the convinced. It was, furthermore, an argument strangely unavailable to the vast majority of fallen mankind outside the chosen West. No act of supernatural revelation or interposition, no message from beyond mortal man, has ever been shown, in any empirically or logically evidential context of inquiry, to be other than the product of the human imagination and of human discourse. The point is as hoary as Xenophanes, the pre-

Socratic: were cattle to postulate a god (perhaps they do), he would have horns and hooves. This insight is reiterated, with a cold fury of reason in Hobbes's *Leviathan* (I, 12): "Men, Women, a Bird, a Crocodile, a Calf, a Dogge, a Snake, an Onion, a Leeke, Deified."

Nor are the motives for such prodigal fantastications in any regard mysterious. Ample spaces for infantilism, for irrationality, for panic and shocks of guilt subsist in the human psyche. Millions, in the scientific-technological West, conduct their daily affairs by astrology. Do not get out of bed on the thirteenth of the month without recourse to touches of exorcism. Regard black cats as vaguely infernal and quake at thunderstorms. We are, as yet, in the nursery of potential evolution. Nanny is simultaneously ached for and dreaded. The notion of cosmic solitude, the admittedly counterintuitive hypothesis of a perfectly aleatory, "meaningless" natural order ("meaningless" in reference to a handful of hominids in a fortuitous corner of an average galaxy), are, to a great majority among us, unbearable. We crave a witness, even fiercely judgmental, to our small dirt. In sickness, in psychological or material terror, when our children lie dead before our eyes, we cry out. That such a cry resounds in nothingness, that it is a perfectly natural, even therapeutic, reflex but nothing more, is almost impossible to endure. Unquestionably, belief in the resurrection of Elvis Presley or prayers at the site of his neon-sepulchre bring solace and roseate hopes to his faithful.

In worldly terms, organized religions have had much to contribute to the horrors of history. Untold generations, ethnic communities, social groups, have been hounded, enslaved, massacred, forcibly converted in the name of doctrinal claims. A tortuous but unmistakable road winds from the medieval pogroms to the Nazi death-camps. Islam has slain since its inception. It is a banal observation that religious wars and the extirpation of heresy via crusades have been among the cruelest and most costly on record. At present, be it in Northern Ireland or Bosnia, in the Middle East or Indonesia, religious-ideological conflicts rage. Atheism knows no heretics, no "holy wars" (an obscene idiom). Nothing from within its private, non-institutionalized structure calls for hatred. By its very nature, it need not proselytize. Such rare instances of "enforced atheism" as in the Stalinist program are a direct imitation, an imbecile parody of the state-church. It cannot, moreover, be demonstrated that the behavior of the believer, under pressure of religious sanctions and rewards, excels that of the atheist or agnostic humanist. Greed and hypocrisy flourish in synagogue-, church-, or mosque-dominated societies. Decency, morality self-imposed, self-generated, are also secular values. Thus, and famously, Ivan Karamazov, when bearing witness to God's non-intervention when an innocent child is being whipped to death (a daily, thousandfold occurrence), gives back to God his "ticket of admission." But there is, to be sure, not a shred of evidence that any such ticket was issued to man in the first place.

These are classic findings. The comprehensiveness, the verifiability and predictive force of Darwinism have added their weight (though obstinate unclarities do persist). As the millennium nears its close, cosmology and astrophysics are providing more and more coherent, experimentally buttressed models of creation. The concept of "beginning" is acquiring its mathematics. To ask what "came before" the nanoseconds of the Big Bang is non-sense. Arguing in an eerily Augustinian vein, cosmologists postulate that time itself only comes into being together with its relevant cosmos – of which there may, very likely, be a boundless multiplicity, each with its own space-time co-ordinates, n-dimensional "strings" of matter and anti-matter, and none privileged by special creation. We keep nagging at this question of "before" only because the general run of human brains is entrapped in an atavistic language-game. Long after Copernicus, we cling to "sunset" and "sunrise." (The landings on the moon *should* have led reason to speak of "earthrise" and "earthset.")

The generation *in vitro* of self-replicating molecules, the manipulation of DNA to planned socio-genetic purposes – the eradication of inherited disease, the cloning of armies – are in reach. These developments will necessitate a thorough revision of our conceptual alphabet. What were, millennially, the building-blocks of all theological and teleological narratives, the deistic postulate of a universal design by some supreme architect, the ascription of a personal, singular destiny, are now being effaced or fundamentally re-thought. What will be the ontological status of human life, of personality, when these are replicated, enhanced, and controlled in the laboratory, in the computerized sperm-bank?

Consciousness is, as yet, an elusive problem. Borrowing, perhaps ironically, from a discarded vocabulary, biochemists, neurophysiologists, geneticists, clinical psychologists refer to the consciousness-problem as the "Holy Grail." It is, today, the eminent target of their quest. The search will take time and genius. But, proclaims a Francis Crick, there is no ground whatever for regarding the challenge as insoluble. In a phrase whose teasing ambiguity and arrogance have entered the language, the sciences, the "theoreticians of everything" are soon to know "the mind of God" (Hawking). Which is to say, they are soon to have a theoretical-experimental understanding of the neurochemical organism which, for primitive, temporal lack of a better story, invented "God." Hobbes, once again: "They invoked also their own Wit, by the name of *Muses;* their own Ignorance, by the name of *Fortune;* their own Lust, by the name of *Cupid;* their own Rage, by

the name of *Furies;* their own privy members, by the name of
Priapus . . ."

I thirst to embrace these sagacities. I am unable to refute them
on their own calm ground. They comport existential consequences which seem to me liberating. Particularly, in respect of
death. In our therapeutic dispensation, the terminally ill, the old
are consuming more and more of the resources, time, and energies
of the young. A piteous gerontocracy lies in the offing. One need
only to have smelt the fear and urine in old-age wards or to have
heard the blind screams of those afflicted with Alzheimer's disease,
to know the hideous waste – it devours not only the patient – of
life artificially sustained. To drift via pain into a vegetable state is
to defile, within oneself, within others, the meaning and worth of
identity. Atheism accords the choice to oneself. No transcendent
party is implicated or empowered. No mystique of pre-ordained
assignment – "God gave me life and only He can decide when that
gift is to be returned" – interposes. What more somber fanaticism
than to keep alive those who would have rest? When the moment
comes, I hope to find my own exit.

In brief, would that I could jettison the archaic language-games
or indeed "speech-pathologies" of a religious worldview. Would
that I could confidently outgrow this "infantile disorder" (Lenin's
phrase, but it could have been Freud's), and ripen into a solely rational, naturalistic order, answerable only to reason and aloneness.

Lists are tedious. They prove nothing. But how, otherwise, can
I clarify my "perplexities" (Maimonides' courteous term)? Any
roll-call of supreme intellect, of rational and analytic capacities far
beyond the norm, must, even if it is limited to the Western tradition, include Socrates, Plato, Aristotle, Augustine, Pascal (in so
many ways a scientific sensibility of the very first rank), Newton,
and Immanuel Kant. Where diagnostic understanding enlists pre-

eminent strengths of the imagination or "proof" via example, our cast would include Dante, Tolstoy, Dostoevsky. There is a documented "God-presence" in the work of a Descartes, an Einstein, a Wittgenstein. But why go on? The point is obvious: the "best that has been thought and formed" in our legacy, with certain signal exceptions (Shakespeare?), draws on, is underwritten by one or another mode and narrative of a divine presence, of a non-empirical dimension to reality. No Bach, no Beethoven, no Michelangelo without such re-insurance. The riposte is no less obvious: these lofty authorities are, increasingly, of the past. Their witness only marks a stage in the evolutionary, progressive biochemistry of *homo* (not yet altogether) *sapiens sapiens*. As Trotsky promised, even an Aristotle or a Goethe are there to be outgrown.

I do see the proud logic of this refutation, but find it defective. In the exact and applied sciences, progress is a verifiable fact. The assertion that I, that anyone, has by mere virtue of social-intellectual context or a very brief lapse of time, capacities for analytic reflection, for insights into the nature of man and of being more ample, more penetrating than (I do not say "different from") those of a Plato, a Dante, or a Pascal, does strike me as dubious in the extreme. As does the correlative ruling that such men and/or women were the victims of a collective delusion, of consensual superstitions, of what logic calls "category mistakes" (the confusion of one language-game for another). The assumption that we have outgrown Spinoza or Kant – though we tell our story differently – leaves me unpersuaded. Arguments from authority are, I know, suspect. (Though they are rife in the sciences also.) But if one is at liberty to choose one's company, that of the believers is of overwhelming distinction. To discard it, to assign to its perceptions a merely rhetorical or antiquarian force, is to leave the greater part of our civilization vacant.

But have not "God's absence" from Auschwitz and the child dying in the cancer-ward done precisely that?

Invoking precedent, intuitively so powerful, logically so null, engages the metaphysics, the art, the literature, the music which have filled my life. It implicates, as well, the inexplicable wonder of certain intimate encounters and relations. Not only in the West has much of the facticity of human constructs – spiritual, material, intellectual – been "for the greater glory of God." *Ad maiorem gloriam Dei.* Aeschylus' *Oresteia* and Plato's *Timaeus;* Job and the Psalms; the temples at Paestum and our cathedrals; Augustine's *Confessions* and the *Commedia;* the Sistine Chapel and the *Missa Solemnis.* Imagine our landscapes without their places of worship; our arts and music without their address to matters of faith; our philosophy and metaphysics, from the pre-Socratics to Heidegger, if they lacked the motion towards, the investigation of, the debate on religious experience, on the first principle or the prime mover. I have already cited Shakespeare as a conceivable, towering exception. There is in his plays a seeming absence of any ascertainable religious position. The "God-question" is, on occasion, tremendously there: in *Lear,* in the veiled parables of salvation throughout the final romances. But we can make out nothing of a *credo* if any.

Elsewhere, the aesthetics, the philosophic discourse in our traditions have been declaring, allegorizing, querying, narrating, at their manifold heart, a "waiting for Godot." Music, above all, is intimately inwoven with this intimation. So much of it is, in a public guise, "sacred." This holds as true of a Bach cantata or a Mozart *Requiem* as it does of a Mahler symphony and a Britten canticle. But the relationship is at once more pervasive and difficult to delineate. In most of us, as I have sought to show, the music we treasure, which inhabits us indispensably, induces a deepening, a receptivity towards emotions which psychologists have called "oceanic." We are "transported," "translated," as humbly, as ecstatically, as was Bottom. But how, and to where? The analogy – it could be much more – with psychosomatic apprehensions of the transcendent, of the insistently inexplicable, is compelling. It has been said that music enacts the prayer of the unbeliever or non-practicing. Yet to whom does it pray?

The parallel can, I think, be made more exact. Music is meaningful to the utmost; it signifies totally. But neither its meanings nor its significations can be verbalized, adequately paraphrased, or translated conceptually into any domain except repeated performance. Logic has no purchase on musical sense. I doubt very much whether neurophysiological hypotheses as to consciousness will ever explicate either the creation of music or its impact upon us. Both of these existential facts, without which, as Nietzsche said, life would be empty, are as empirically manifest, as transformative of being as any known to human experience. Yet they seem to lie outside analytic-experimental understanding.

The very same intractabilities of the self-evident characterize the signifying "non-sense" of theological and liturgical propositions. It may be that such propositions embody a frustrated endeavor to transcribe into the constricted code of linear grammatical statements necessities of feeling, of intuition which are in some radical sphere "musical." What I remain confident of is this: should the question of the existence or non-existence of God lapse into triviality, should it drain out of our private and public awareness like ancient, muddied waters, thought and the totality of the arts as we have known them will alter. They may, after opaque, turbulent movements of transition, come to tell altogether new, unprecedented stories and produce world-images of which we can, at present, have little prevision. Already, there are those, like Foucault, who profess the end of authorship, of individual begetting, indeed of the persona of man. It seems more modest and plausible to suppose that what may not recur, in the absence of the God-question and its metaphors, are certain formal and executive magnitudes of metaphysical and aesthetic realization. The overarching constructs of felt order, as we find them in Dante, in a Bach *Passion*, in the critiques of Kant or the frescoes of Giotto, but also in the concise parables of Kafka, whose briefest syllable is charged with a "sickness unto God," may be of the past.

But neither the good company one is in as a believer, nor the primacy in our inheritance of the religious precedent, are probative. I take the very project of proving the existence of God rationally, argumentatively to be misguided. Even the subtlest of so-called ontological proofs – that of Anselm, which an astonished Bertrand Russell regarded as logically impeccable, that of Descartes or of Schelling – are only pieces of mental-grammatological play. Kant was perfectly right in characterizing all proofs of reason in reference to God as a blind alley. Indeed, what would God be if His being could be circumscribed, let alone demonstrated by human dialectics and ratiocination? Belief is not evidential except in the naïvest, fundamentally sentimental vein – for example, by appeal to the "grandeur and glory" of the natural world or to personal well-being or need. On the evidence available to human reason and empirical investigation, there can be only one honest answer: the agnostic "I do not know"; "I do not know either way." Such agnosticism, fractured by impulses of anguished prayer, of unthinking cries to "God" in moments of terror and of suffering, is ubiquitous in the post-Darwinian, post-Nietzschean, and post-Freudian West. Conscious or not, agnosticism is the established church of modernity. By its somewhat bleak light, the educated and the rational conduct their immanent lives. To underline: agnosticism is not atheism. Atheism, where it is consequently held and lived, is a journey completed, a disciplined homecoming to nothingness (Sartre's *l'être et le néant*).

A specific agnosticism in respect of reason or "proof" lies at the base of my own fragmentary and disheveled convictions. I feel assured that if "God" exists, He/She – as current courtesies demand – can have nothing whatever in common with the conceptions of Him/Her advanced by human minds, however acute. Abstract, metaphysically cunning as these conceptions may be, the speculations, or the grammars of the men and women who have articulated them remain ineluctably anthropomorphic. They are fatally bounded by the cerebral synapses, by the metaphoric and analogical means of our psyche. They hover, with greater or lesser sophistication, in the aura of that majestic, bearded *pater familias* (so oddly resembling Karl Marx) imagined for the common run of mankind on the Sistine ceiling. There is far more affinity between the mind of a child and, say, the general theory of relativity than between the most penetrating intellect and the "nature," whatever that may signify, of "God." The remove comes nearest to any comprehensible definition of infinity. The totem, the idol of wood or stone, is wholly honest in its figurative limitations. So, at a more strenuously didactic level, was the total emptiness of the Holy of Holies in the temple at Jerusalem. But even this emptiness is nothing but a picture, a "black on black." It says nothing of "God." Hence my attempts to adhere to the suggestion offered in certain "negative theologies" and metaphysics. I sense that "God" can be addressed inwardly only as *the totally Other*; that there are no definitional means or translations into "us." "In that case," challenges the agnostic or the atheist, "what difference does it make? If the totally 'Other' is inaccessible to human reason or imagination, if the notion of His/Its concern with our petty and grimy lives is infantile nonsense, why bother?"

The question is eminently just. I can only reply by force of unreason, by appeal to intuitions as to the boundary conditions and deficiencies of rationality and the empirical. The often unexamined arrogance of reason, notably in the sciences, seems to me to cut off ascertainable experience from what may be essential. It is to know everything, but to know nothing else. Nothing in science or logical discourse can either resolve or ostracize Leibniz's question of all questions: "Why is there not nothing?" The positivist edict whereby an adult consciousness will only ask of the world and of existence "How?" and not "Why?" is censorship of the most obscurantist kind. It would gag the voice beneath voices within us. Even on the "How?" level, it is by no means certain that the majestic sciences will find demonstrable answers. There is an embarrassing evasion and sophistry to the ruling, to which I have already adverted, that it is somehow illicit or childish to inquire about time before time, about the nanosecond before the Big Bang. There is for me so undeniable a pressure of presence extraterritorial to explanation (music being the everyday, yet unfathomable, analogue to just this pressure of presence).

Nevertheless, the challenge persists. How can "the totally Other" act on us, let alone give any signal of its utterly inaccessible existence?

The ultimate "particles," the bondings of elements in human consciousness whose orbits generate the quantum jump of faith, are presumably multiple. They are not unambiguously accountable to even the masters of introspection, of self-decoding, such as Pascal or Kierkegaard. They sink their roots into the finalities of the unconscious. Childhood experiences (according to Freud, this is where the discussion should stop) are seminal. Each atom of time in our life-histories can be causal either way. Belief or non-belief are closely resonant, thought at depths of intricacy that defy analysis, with our immersion and dissatisfactions with language. If God speaks being into being, we in turn speak or deny God verbally (what is the prayer of the deaf-mute?). Tradition, the purposefully irrational and formal regimen of daily ritual, as in orthodox Judaism, may stand for an assent to God. Injustice, motiveless catastrophe – that earthquake in Lisbon which traumatized the deists of the Enlightenment – can eradicate faith. Some men and women are shaped by the potter's hand of the apostolic, of the teacher; others bite it. The genesis in any individual of a sense of God or of a non-sense is precisely as diverse, as complex and resistant to transparent summation as is individuation itself. The trigger for or against, the leap in or out, belong to the chemistry of the unknown. I can testify only to symptoms, a medical term wonderfully apposite to those *krank an Gott.*

When I am confronted, via reports, pictures, personal notice, of the infliction of wanton pain on children and on animals, a despairing rage floods me. There are those who tear out the eyes of living children, who shoot children in the eyes, who beat animals across their eyes. These facts overwhelm me with desolate loathing. The hatred, the despair they unleash in me are far in excess of my mental and nervous resources. The hot blackness I feel engulfed in transcends my will. I am possessed by enormity. But this despairing hatred and grief, this nausea of soul, have a strange counter-echo. I don't know how else to put it. At the maddening center of despair is the insistent instinct – again, I can put it no other way – of a broken contract. Of an appalling and specific cataclysm. In the futile scream of the child, in the mute agony of the tortured animal, sounds the "background noise" of a horror after creation, after being torn loose from the logic and repose of nothingness. Something – how helpless language can be – has gone hideously wrong. Reality should, could have been otherwise (the "Other"). The phenomenality of organic, conscious existence should, could have made impossible the sadism, the unending hurt of our ways. The impotent fury, the guilt which master and surpass my identity carry with them the working hypothesis, the "working metaphor," if you will, of "original sin."

To this expression, I am unable to attach any reasoned, let alone historical substance. On the pragmatic-narratological plane, stories of some initial crime and inherited culpability are universal fables – uncannily profound and lasting. Nothing more. Yet in the presence of the beaten, raped child, of the horse or mule flogged across its eyes, I am possessed, as by a midnight clarity, by the intuition of the Fall. Only some such happening, irretrievable to reason, can make intelligible, though always near to unbearable, the actualities of our history on this wasted earth. We are condemned to be our cruel, greedy, egotistical, mendacious selves. When it was, when it must have been meant to be *otherwise*. When the truth and self-sacrificial compassion of exceptional men and women show so plainly what might have been. I have found myself wondering, fantasticating childishly, whether human history is not the passing nightmare of a sleeping god. Whether He will not wake from it so as to render unnecessary, once and for all, the scream of the child, the gagging of the beaten animal.

Love is the dialectic of hatred, its mirror-opposite. Love is, in varying intensities, the imperative wonder of the irrational. It is non-negotiable, as is the (condemned) search for God among His infirm. To shake, in one's inmost spirit, nerve, and bone, at the sight, at the voice, at the merest touch of the beloved; to contrive, to labor, to lie without end so as to reach, to be near the man or woman loved; to transform one's existence – personal, public, psychological, material – on an unforeseen instant, in the cause and consequence of love; to undergo unspeakable hurt and blankness at the absence of the beloved one, at the withering of love; to identify the divine with the emanation of love, as does all Platonism, which is to say, the Western model of transcendence – is to partake of the most commonplace and inexplicable sacrament in human life. It is, within one's personal potential, to touch the ripeness of the spirit. To equate this universe of experience with the libidinal, as does Freud, to account for it in terms of biogenetic, procreative advantages, are reductions almost contemptible. Love can be the unchosen bond, to the pitch of self-destruction, between individuals blatantly unsuited to each other. Sexuality can be incidental, transient, or altogether absent. The ugly, the wretched, the most evil among us can be the object of disinterested, impassioned eros. The desire to die for the beloved or the friend – *l'amie*, as French so exactly and luminously has it – the clear-eyed insanities of jealousy, are counter-productive on any conceivable biological (Darwinian) or social reckoning. The celebrated Pascalian maxim whereby the heart has its reasons which reason does not know, plays defensively on rationality. It is not "reasons" which crowd the heart. It is necessities of a wholly different provenance. Beyond reason, beyond good and evil, beyond sexuality which, even at the crest of ecstasy, is so minor and ephemeral an act. I have stood through a rain-sodden night to catch a glimpse of the beloved turning a corner. Perhaps it was not even she. God have mercy on those who have never known the hallucination of light which fills the dark during such a vigil.

From the unreasoned, unanalyzable, often ruinous all-power of love stems the thought – is it, once more, a puerility? – that "God" is not yet. That He will come into being or, more precisely, into manifest reach of human perception, only when there is immense excess of love over hatred. Each and every cruelty, each and every injustice inflicted on man or beast justifies the findings of atheism insofar as it prevents God from what would indeed be a first coming. But I am unable, even at the worst hours, to abdicate from the belief that the two validating wonders of mortal existence are love and the invention of the future tense. Their conjunction, if it will ever come to pass, is the Messianic.

"He who thinks greatly must err greatly," said Martin Heidegger, the parodist-theologian of our age (where "parodist" is meant in its gravest sense). Also those who "think small" may err greatly. This is the democracy of grace, or of damnation.

Index

Titles with dates are the works of the author.

Heine, Heinrich 10, 59
Hellenic polytheism 64
Heraclitus 3
Herder, Johann Gottfried von 102
hermeneutics 19, 22, 27, 171
Hiroshima 121
Hispanic communities 88
histories 107
Hitler, Adolf 8, 11, 54, 55, 62–63, 68
"Hitler and the IXth Symphony; *Seit umzingelt Millionen*" 70
Hitlerite-Stalinist persecution 56
Hobbes, Thomas 177, 179–80
"Homer" 17
Hölderlin, Johann 41, 111, 132
Holocaust 54, 57, 68, 118, 167
Homer 18–19, 25, 174
  Iliad 14–19
  Odyssey 16–17, 21, 113
Homer in English (1996) 17
homicidal herd-reflexes 123
Hong Kong 168
hope 95
Hopkins, Gerard Manley 3, 74, 112, 143
House, Humphry 143–44
Housman, Alfred Edward 138
humaneness 122
humanistic-academic studies 108–9
humans
  brains, languages 107
  capacity to perform 171
  consciousness 83–84
  history 188
  speech 78–79
Humboldt, Baron von 47
hunger 115
Hunnish incursions 115

Husserl, Edmund 39
Hutchins, Robert Maynard 45

Ibsen, Henrik Johan 79
Icelandic tundra 169
ideologies 61, 93, 102, 121
idioms 97
"if" sentences 95
impatience 172
In Bluebeard's Castle (1971) 63
incomprehension 92
Indian Ocean 168
Indian tongue 98
individual and social conditions 116
Indonesia 178
  mass-murders 119
industrial revolution 116
Ingres, Jean 25
inheritance 127
Inquisition 55, 57
interlingual translations 105–6
Internet 128, 133
interpretation 24–25
Ireland
  literature and arts 130
  Northern 119, 178
Isaac 55, 57, 60, 176
Isaac the Blind 165, 166
Isaiah 62
Islam 57, 135, 159
Israel 53–54, 59–60, 62, 66, 119, 174
Italian, language 101
Italy, north-east, trilingualism 88
Ithaka 168

Jacob 55
Jakobson, Roman 97

CPSIA information can be obtained at www.ICGtesting.com
Printed in the USA
BVOW03s0712050314

346664BV00002BA/36/P